THE BEATLES

GET BACK

BY THE BEATLES

Featuring photography by Ethan A. Russell and Linda McCartney

Foreword by Peter Jackson

Introduction by Hanif Kureishi

Edited by John Harris from transcripts of the original sound recordings

Apple   CALLAWAY

London and New York
2021

Note to the reader

The text primarily consists of conversations between The Beatles and their associates that took place during the *Get Back* sessions
throughout January 1969. These have been carefully transcribed and edited from the original Nagra sound recordings.

Images with rectangular borders are photographs taken during the sessions by Ethan A. Russell or Linda McCartney
(unless otherwise specified on page 239). Images with round-cornered borders are film frames from the original 16mm footage,
every frame digitally scanned and restored as part of the process of creating the movie *The Beatles: Get Back* that this book accompanies.

THE BEATLES: GET BACK by THE BEATLES © 2021 Apple Corps Limited

Published by
CALLAWAY ARTS & ENTERTAINMENT
41 Union Square West, Suite 1101, New York, New York 10003
and
APPLE CORPS LIMITED
27 Ovington Square, London SW3 1LJ

Visit Callaway at www.callaway.com
Visit The Beatles at www.thebeatles.com

ISBN: 978-0-935112-96-2

First Edition, First Printing
Printed and bound in Italy by Tecnostampa—Pigini Group Printing Division
Distributed in the US, Canada, the UK and Ireland by Ingram Publisher Services
www.ingramcontent.com

Library of Congress Cataloguing-in-Publication data is available.

The paper in this book is made from sustainably managed forests and controlled sources.
PEFC™ Certified PEFC/18-31-260

CONTENTS

FOREWORD

PETER JACKSON

I was born in 1961, so I would have been seven or eight years old when the events detailed in this compelling book took place. I've been digging into the depths of my memory, trying to dig up some contemporaneous memory of 1969… of 'Get Back'… of *Let It Be*… of The Beatles… of anything at all!

I did have a tiny bit of luck in the memory department.

You see, I was an only child and my parents were comparatively old. They had a gramophone and a record collection that consisted of around thirty LPs. Their favourites were things like the soundtrack of *South Pacific*. My mum got into the Sixties groove with a short, sharp adoration for Engelbert Humperdinck. My favourite record was *Tennessee Ernie Ford sings Civil War Songs of the North*. I remember my dad arriving home with that record, and I was always slightly annoyed that he didn't get *Songs of the South* at the same time.

I grew up with no Beatles records, and no access to them… until one night, which must have been in 1970, when Dad arrived home from work, having just bought a 45rpm single. I remember it looked kind of weird being so small. He'd fallen in love with a song he'd heard on the radio called 'Something' – so much so, he had actually bought the single. It was the one and only time he ever had that impulse.

So 'Something' was played in our house over and over again. I started to hear Shirley Bassey's voice in my dreams. Yes, it was Shirley Bassey's cover of the Beatles single, and the closest I ever came to growing up with a Beatles record.

But I must have heard them on the radio, and liked them. I remember my mum talking about The Beatles, and how my cousins had been to their concert in Wellington. She claimed to have liked them, 'until they got all weird and became hippies'.

Around the time I was twelve or thirteen, I figured out a way to earn some decent money. Before dawn, I'd head off up into the very steep hills that surrounded Pukerua Bay, the little town I grew up in, with a knife and bucket. I'd spend hours scrambling up and down in search of little patches of enormous flat mushrooms – the type we call 'Portobello' today.

Arriving home with a bucketful, I'd pack them into paper bags (broken ones at the bottom, perfect ones on top), and stand on the side

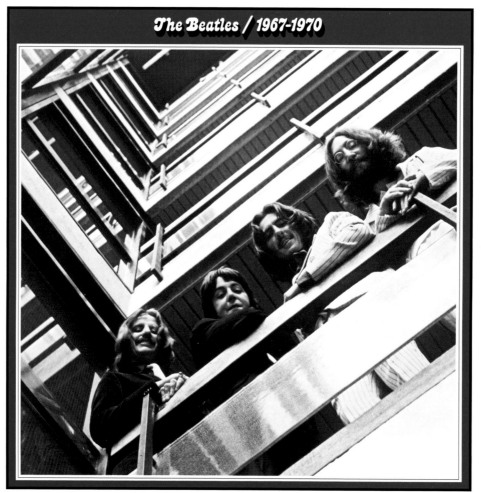

of New Zealand's main highway with a sign, selling them for 10c a bag. I made some serious money, which let me jump on the train into Wellington. I was heading for the big hobby store to buy a huge plastic model aircraft that I'd craved for quite some time. But on the way to the hobby store, my plans kind of derailed…

I passed a record store that had a window display showing two 'new' Beatles albums – one with a red cover, the other a blue cover. On the red album cover were the four Beatles in their young mop-top days, and on the blue album, in exactly the same pose, were the bearded hippy Beatles that my mother had warned me about. I stopped dead and looked at the song listings. Although I only recognised a handful of titles, those brilliant album covers had snagged me.

Needless to say, I blew my model aircraft money on those two double albums and got back on the train with what, I came to learn later, were the most wonderful songs I've ever heard, tucked under my arm.

That's how my Beatles story began… and in the decades following, the musical genius of John Lennon, Paul McCartney, George Harrison and Ringo Starr went on and *'changed my life in oh so many ways'*, to borrow their own words.

With the release of this book, and our accompanying movie, there'll be plenty written about the circumstances around The Beatles' *Get Back* project of January 1969. I don't intend to go into that story here, but I'll just say something about the massive amount

of historic material filmed and recorded by Michael Lindsay-Hogg and his crew.

For decades, outside of the *Let It Be* movie, the huge amount of out-takes have only been available on bootleg audio. I had some of these, and the experience of listening to the sub-standard sound is tough. It's created a negative impression for sure.

When I was lucky enough to watch all of the movie footage, matched to the sound, it was an utterly different experience, as you'll see in our movie.

And then when Apple Corps told me about this book, based on the transcribed audio conversations, I must admit I was dubious. 'Really? A book isn't going to have moving images, it isn't going to have songs to listen to. Is that a good idea?'

But the first time I read the book you hold in your hands, I realised how wrong I was. It's an entirely different way to present the *Get Back* story, and equally compelling. The true spirit of the *Get Back* sessions is captured in these pages – just look at the number of times the description 'laughing' is used. Over and over again, there amongst the beautiful photographs by Ethan Russell and Linda McCartney.

I wouldn't have written this introduction if I had walked straight past the record store and bought myself that model aircraft, back in the early 1970s. So I'd like to say one thing to little thirteen-year-old 'PJ'…

Thanks, mate.

INTRODUCTION: ALL YOU NEED

HANIF KUREISHI

When I think about The Beatles, I like to consider an interesting if not provocative statement: 'No masterpiece was ever produced by several people together.' This is said by a character in *The Counterfeiters*, by French novelist André Gide.

Clearly, Gide wasn't pondering movies, or architecture, or newspapers, or popular music from Liverpool. And even if we contemplate the great 'soloists' of our time, like Picasso, do we not have to include in the picture his colleagues and contemporaries? These were poets, philosophers and composers, as well as painters like Matisse and Braque, with whom the great soloist conducted a running dialogue. As with the four Beatles, the respect and rivalry of this close-knit gang made each of them better artists. They too were 'roped together for the climb', as Picasso put it about Braque.

When I – a mixed-race boy, brought up in a rough, lower-middle-class London suburb after the war – dream of this group of friends and collaborators, The Beatles, they remind me of everything I love about Britain. That love is for the exhilarating, dissenting art that comes from its young people. When I think about The Beatles, which I do every day – I sit down and play one song all through in the morning, before starting work, to ignite my mood – I dream of magic, stardust and variety, of lightness, charm and *joie de vivre*. And I often wonder how this sunshine seemed to break out one fine day in the 1960s.

If you want to understand how people and systems break down, you can learn a lot by studying how creative partnerships like those of The Beatles do work, how they develop, and how brilliant collaborators can together make something extraordinary where there was nothing before, through a kind of play. You could call this Eros, a form of pleasurable, creative making, the best kind of enjoyable work. But it is unusual for the outsider, the passionate observer, to have a chance to witness this kind of labour. Normally, we only see the artist's polished outcome; the struggle, the early sketches and drafts, remain private.

But here, in the film and accompanying book *Get Back*, we have a fly-on-the-wall opportunity. This is the only time in their career that The Beatles were filmed at such length while in the studio creating. It is a privilege and an opportunity to see them chatting and improvising, in close-up, in their everydayness. These are young people, don't forget, in their mid to late twenties, three of whom have known each other since school, and who have collectively made music together most days since. Like us they gossip, joke, argue, split up, get back together. Most importantly – they work together.

These four non-posh Liverpool boys worked a lot. They rarely stopped, or had a day off. 'The White Album' had been released in November 1968. Here they are again, in this new story, from 2 January 1969, at Twickenham Film Studios in West London, where they would be filmed by Michael Lindsay-Hogg, the director who had made the 'Hey Jude' video.

There they intend to rehearse for a proposed live gig, and work on what became the *Let It Be* album. They also develop some of the brilliant songs – 'Something', 'She Came In Through The Bathroom Window', 'Carry That Weight', 'I Want You (She's So Heavy)' and 'Octopus's Garden' – which would later appear on the George Martin-produced *Abbey Road*. Although they are preparing to play live again – maybe while travelling to North Africa on an ocean liner, playing on Primrose Hill, or perhaps on Gibraltar – they can't agree as to where or how this event would take place. They do know, at least, that Ringo doesn't want to go abroad; he doesn't like the food.

Fortunately for us, this process was recorded on two Nagra tape recorders. There are over 120 hours of it. As well as the music, these tapes contain the conversations between songs by all the band and the crew (although we hear slightly less from Ringo than from the others because his drums weren't always miked).

It's sometimes assumed that this was a sad or grim time for the band, that they were falling apart, unhappy, and no longer really wanted to work together. There were indeed disputes and differences, as there would be with any group of artists. But in fact this was a productive time for them, when they created some of their best work. And it is here that we have the privilege of witnessing their early drafts, the mistakes, the drift and digressions, the boredom, the excitement, joyous jamming and sudden breakthroughs that led to the work we now know and admire.

If you grew up, as I did, after the war in the 1950s, then your notion of culture was bewildering: being taken, for instance, around an endless, unexplained art gallery and being made to listen to Tchaikovsky. The message was clear: culture, whatever it was, was above our heads. We were not people it was made for. Not that we were not already sceptical of adults, who, from where we were looking, seemed mostly to lead dull, unenviable lives. If school was anything to go by, adults seemed to fear and envy young people, when they were not deriding or disparaging them. What was supposed to be appealing to us in the future – the idea of becoming a working adult with a family – just didn't look that desirable.

Yet all the time, young people – particularly if they had heard Elvis or Little Richard – were yearning for art they could understand in terms of the frustration and snowballing sexuality of their lives. An art that would speak for and about them, giving them a reason to be excited about the future. After all, belief in the future is a precious commodity. It is not something you can acquire alone. You need a group, a movement, a shared culture.

And then, suddenly, it was there. It existed. It was happening, in our country.

Britain, having begun to recover from the war, and wondering what sort of place it wanted to be, was being reborn as a country of culture. There were these young faces – The Beatles and others – with strange and fascinating hair on television and in newspapers and magazines; and the music they made was on the radio. Somewhere – mostly in London, but not only in London – there was social mobility, the possibility of escape, and of a fuller future. And it wasn't one of Britain's public schools or great universities which produced these revolutionary boys. It was a war-ruined and ravaged port city in the North.

The Beatles, these artists who were by far the best of all the talent around, were like us, both ordinary and extraordinary, from nowhere and going somewhere – everywhere! Even in the suburbs we were aware the kids were taking over. On the bus to school in the morning you might witness a terrifying parade: there would be Teds, mods, rockers, skins and, a bit later, hippies. It was a meritocratic moment.

CALL SHEET

No. Studio 1.

PRODUCTION NAME :-	"APPLE RECORDS 1"	PROD. No. :- Apple Films Ltd.
STAFF CALL :- 8.30 a.m. on Stage 1.		CALL FOR DATE :- Thursday, 2nd January, 1969.
SETS OR LOCATIONS :-	INT. RECORDING STUDIO.	

ARTISTES	DRESSING ROOM No.	CHARACTER	TIME REQUIRED AT STUDIO	TIME REQUIRED ON SET
JOHN LENNON	Apt.1 & 2.		10.00 a.m.	
PAUL McCARTNEY	" "		10.00 a.m.	
GEORGE HARRISON	" "		10.00 a.m.	
RINGO STARR	" "		10.00 a.m.	

Props: 6 chairs and table required.

Canteen: a.m. and p.m. Tea Breaks for 24 people please.

Lunch: 1.00 - 2.00 p.m.

Sound Requirements: 2 Nagras
                        2 Neck Microphones
                        1 Rifle microphone

Camera Requirements: 2 Complete 16 m.m. B.L. outfits

Music and Equipment: As arranged with Mel Evans.

Unit: Producer   Denis O'Dell
            Director   Michael Lindsay-Hogg
            Cameraman   Tony Richmond
            Asst.Director   Ray Freeborn
            Operator   Les Parrot
            Clapper/Loader Paul Bond
            Gaffer   Jim Powell
            Sound Mixer   Peter Sutton
            Boom Operator   Ken Reynolds
            3 Electricians
            Propman   Alf Pegley
Transport for Artistes as arranged.

Processing: Humphries Labs, Contact: Mr. Freddie Grey

Brian Epstein

From now on, it looked like anyone could try to be an artist: in music, fashion, photography, theatre, movies or writing. It had all opened up. As British kids, until The Beatles, we never knew what we were supposed to be proud of. But once The Beatles arrived, and Britain was at the forefront of a cultural revolution led by young people, London, in particular, was becoming a world city of art, a catwalk, a crucible, a party where you wore what you wanted, and where anything could happen.

Unlike us, The Beatles had busy lives and most days we wondered what they were doing, and, more importantly, what they were thinking. Not that it was difficult to find out. For a while, fame suited them. Maureen Cleave stated in the *Evening Standard*, in March 1966, 'They are famous in the way the Queen is famous. When John Lennon's Rolls-Royce, with its black wheels and its black windows, goes past, people say: "It's the Queen," or "It's The Beatles." With her they share the security of a stable life.'

Why would they object to being looked at? We were learning to become consumers, and we consumed The Beatles, who were very

consumable. We couldn't get enough. They were, after all, beautiful, desirable, clever and funny, and were forever being photographed somewhere or other, looking sexy and cool. And the music that poured from them so prolifically in a kind of Mozartian flow always seemed effortless. For a start, they weren't coerced into producing it, as we felt coerced and intimidated at school. It was obvious they loved what they did.

What they were up to, and their humour confirms it, was playing. And it is in play, so the psychologists tell us, and Jung in particular – who appeared on the cover of *Sgt. Pepper* – that we are at our most human. Play is where nothing is unthinkable, unimaginable or mocked. Play is dynamic, creative, experimental, it is always open to the new. The child makes and remakes the world, taking control of it, exerting a magical mastery over it. A child who couldn't play would be in trouble. Something would be stuck.

The point was: there were four of them, along with manager Brian Epstein and producer George Martin. Despite the dominance of the idea of the romantic, solitary genius, such

George Martin

collaborative magic has happened before. There have been more partnerships in art than stolid old André Gide could imagine. Think of the creative friendship and enmity between Coleridge and Wordsworth, when 'to be young was very heaven'; of Pound urging Eliot to crop large sections of *The Waste Land*; of Vita Sackville-West stirring Virginia Woolf's body and imagination so that she could write *Orlando*; and of Hitchcock and his producer Selznick making Hitchcock's perverse and strange art box-office gold.

Those four Beatle boys were more than good for one another. And 'snags', as Patricia Highsmith calls them in her wonderful book about writing, *Plotting and Writing Suspense Fiction*, or what we might call 'problems in art', have – she insists – to be solved practically, in the room, not in someone's mind. This is where you need severe criticism and/or encouragement.

It takes a lot of trust and nerve to sing or play a new song in front of someone else. You would need to believe your companions would hear you without mockery, that you were in a welcoming environment. You would also

have to believe that exchange and influence is replenishing, nurturing even, and that the other person is not only good for you, but that they will improve and enthuse you. They could change you significantly, in a kind of mutual metamorphosis, or productive encounter. If you're going to argue, you'd want to argue with the right people. Some disagreements can be fruitful or even inspirational. Art is a flux and dialogue, not only with the past, but with the present, with what others are doing. As Charles Darwin wrote, 'It is the long history of humankind (and animal kind, too) that those who learned to collaborate and improvise most effectively have prevailed.'

It is this dialogue of friends we will witness here. Once the group stopped touring and they could concentrate in the studio, their music reached a new level, developing from album to album. As songwriters, The Beatles mostly wrote separately at this time. But they could only have worked with one another in mind, later transforming one another's ideas. They would be one another's convivial, useful critics, mates who would help you produce work you couldn't make alone. To become yourself you need other people.

My parents and I had loved Cliff Richard and even The Shadows; we adored Tommy Steele, who apparently had the good fortune to live nearby in Catford, South London. But there wasn't much originality or freshness to love in most of the British music I grew up with. My father, a Muslim growing up in Bombay, had become enthralled by American writers like Ernest Hemingway, Raymond Chandler and James M. Cain; by American movies and style, particularly raincoats like Bogart's. And when Dad moved to the London suburbs and started a family, there was something new for us from America. We found we were listening to Chuck Berry and Fats Domino on the radio.

By 1964 what a scene and excitement it had become, even for us, people who led conventional, well-behaved lives with ordinary, if not small, dreams. I was astonished to see my own mother screaming at The Beatles in Bromley Odeon – indeed, many of the mothers of my friends, a line of them in the cheap seats, with their hands clapped to their cheeks and their mouths open like in Munch's *Scream*. Women were not supposed to behave like this.

I'd never seen such passion in mothers before. Those Beatle boys, who wrote songs about men desiring women, were certainly doing something to women who thought of themselves as 'housewives'.

The Beatles did a lot for us. And here they were, bringing in the rest of the world. They were provincial British, English even, but they were never insular: there was always something international, or cosmopolitan, about them. Their Liverpudlian manager Brian Epstein had always felt like an outsider. A failure at school, he'd wanted to be a dress designer. It was his strongest wish. But his father didn't consider it a 'manly' occupation. The Beatles had been seen hanging about in his shop – 'they were not very tidy and not very clean' – and, after seeing them in the Cavern, Epstein signed them up.

The suits he persuaded the formerly scruffy and leather-clad Beatles to wear made them look French or what we used to call Continental. They resembled Alain Delon or Jean-Paul Belmondo in moody thrillers about good-looking, stubbornly original people, who weren't prepared to fit into the straight

world. The Beatles were not only musicians, they had what became known as an Image. They were always at the very pinnacle of style, and their visual sense was strong. Their album covers, as well as their great movie *A Hard Day's Night*, looked like art works. The Beatles weren't just ahead of the wave, they were the wave.

As if to confirm their originality, more snobbish adults didn't get The Beatles at all. Noel Coward wrote in his diary in 1965, '… on the Sunday night, I went to see the Beatles. I had never seen them in the flesh before. The noise was deafening throughout ... I was truly horrified and shocked by the audience. It was like a mass masturbation orgy.'

The aliveness of teenagers can be terrifying. But if older people looked down on 'beat' music this was all right with us. If teenagers agree about wanting one thing, they don't want to be closed in, or understood. But you can see from the numerous television interviews The Beatles did, particularly in America, how patronised and belittled they were, and not taken seriously as artists. Pop was supposed to be as throwaway as

advertising, and as permanent as candyfloss. A year later no one would remember those songs. Or want to hear them again.

Why did they seem so fresh? Outside of pop, the highbrow, war-stained culture of the early '60s was heavy with history. It was deliberately difficult and obscure, as far from the market as it could get. It was intellectual: you'd have to know a lot to make it out. In music there was Morton Feldman, in literature Samuel Beckett and Alain Robbe-Grillet, and in art there was Mark Rothko. This art was sublime. But it was not easy, popular or uplifting. In some ways it was deliberately frustrating, anti-hedonistic. It wasn't afraid of being boring; it wasn't committed to the market.

For me the question was: how could you put your love for The Beatles together with your fascination with *Waiting for Godot?* In what way might they be similar? How to understand it? One day I discovered a copy of Susan Sontag's essay collection *Against Interpretation* in a second-hand bookshop in Bromley. (This was a time when there were several bookshops in the town.)

What had struck me was a photograph on the cover of the volume. Wow, I thought, who is this? It was indeed the author, a ravishing dark-haired young woman, looking like an intelligent model.

And what she was telling us was mind-blowing. Sontag isn't condescending. She mentions The Supremes; she's telling us that Style wasn't just the box, it was what was inside the box too. Style itself was art; the popular was serious, and the serious could be a bit frivolous, like Duchamp, or playful like Picasso, and popular like Hitchcock. The Look was all. It was Style, not morality, that mattered when it came to art. Works of art simply exist. They just are; they don't have to be deep. She talks about 'intelligence, grace and sensuousness'. Then she mentions The Beatles, along with Jean-Luc Godard and the great Italian director Michelangelo Antonioni, an acquaintance of Paul McCartney's. The Fabs had it. Everything had already changed.

To me, this was a revelation. Our education had tried to teach us that real art, even when it was boring, should morally improve you, make you a better person, cultured, aware, more fastidious, with a posher accent even. Education would show you the way. The authorities never stopped telling us what to attend to, what really mattered and what was worthless. What was called culture was always highly regulated and policed. The boundaries were supervised. You crossed them at your peril. If the borders fell, there would be chaos, wouldn't there? The 1950s had, after all, been an era of postwar scarcity, and art was scarce too. Not everyone could have it. Not everyone could understand it. Not you. Not your class or type.

But we'd stopped listening to the authorities. We knew by now that the cinema – formerly considered cheap entertainment – was considered to be art. We'd heard Elvis and now we'd discovered The Rolling Stones, The Beatles, The Kinks and The Who. They'd led us to bodies and to pleasure, and shown us what gratification art could effortlessly deliver. And the authorities – indeed most people – were suspicious of pleasure, and of

any art like Pop that appeared to dispense unmediated good times and desire. Pleasure was a kind of sex, after all, and sex, let's say, could be a slippery slope.

Almost all art for young people was produced by adults, mediated by adults, and approved by them. Adults, apparently, knew what young people need, and what would be good for them. The kids had no say in it. But now they did. The Beatles were at the forefront of this revolution. If there was to be taste and fine distinctions, pop – the stuff we loved and danced to – was considered far below that. It barely counted as important on the scale of art. Again, that had changed: art was pictures and music. We were free.

Then, one day, as we all know, it became clear that this charmed collaboration had become a burden if not a limitation. It began to fall apart.

During the break between 'The White Album' and the *Let It Be* sessions, George Harrison had been in Woodstock, NY, with Bob Dylan, whom he adored and admired. Harrison had worked with Dylan, as well as with The Band, jamming, writing, and teaching Dylan new chords. In 1968 he and Dylan had written 'I'd Have You Anytime' together, later released on *All Things Must Pass*. Music was changing, becoming simpler, less psychedelic and experimental. It had entered a new period, more sincere and rootsy.

On his return to Britain, Harrison disliked the cavernous, inhospitable Twickenham studios. Something had started to change in him. He and Dylan had been equals, working together. With Lennon and McCartney, he had been a younger brother. Through his adolescence and young manhood, he had hidden himself behind that double-flower, where he was protected but also overlooked. He did have, after all, two older brothers. Being the younger one was a natural position for him. In some relationships, you might want to disguise or hide your talent because it threatens others. But this became the childhood he had to leave behind. The son was, indeed, coming.

Billy Preston

We can hear the strain. During the *Let It Be* sessions it is George Harrison who says, 'Ever since Mr Epstein passed away… it's never been the same.' Paul agrees. He can see it too. 'We've been very negative since Mr Epstein passed away. I mean, you know, that's why all of us in turn has been sick of the group, you know, 'cos there's nothing positive in it. You know, it is a bit of a drag. But the only way for it not to be a bit of a drag is for the four of us to think, Should we make it positive?'

It does become positive. Once they move to their own studio, in the basement of Apple at 3 Savile Row, everyone cheers up. There is a burst of creativity before they appear on the roof a week later. Another electrifying element had been added: Billy Preston. Preston, who had first met The Beatles in Hamburg in 1962, was recording a TV special for the BBC, and was invited to join in by George Harrison. 'I feel much better since Billy came, because I feel as though he's doing fills which…' Paul: 'That we should have been doing, yeah.' George adds, ''Cos sometimes it's like… any time there's a space missing.'

During this time they work on several songs simultaneously: 'Don't Let Me Down', 'I've Got A Feeling', 'Get Back' and others. In the transcripts we see them evolve. We can pinpoint the exact moment when Ringo suddenly finds the shuffling beat in 'Get Back', so essential to the classic song we know and love.

At one point during the sessions George Martin says to John Lennon, 'You're writing all the time, aren't you, John?' to which John replies, 'Sure I am.' Later, George Martin comments, 'You're looking at each other, you're seeing each other, you're… just *happening* [clicks fingers].'

After a discussion about the best place to buy comfortable black slip-ons, there's a lovely section when they all get down to work on 'Something' together. Harrison says he's already been working on it for six months, without getting any further. Now they all toss in suggestions for words and lines. Harrison remembers that a while ago, Lennon had given him good advice: that you should finish a song once you've started, presumably before you forget what inspired it. Naturally Lennon doesn't take his own advice. But now he says that, to keep the song moving, you should say any line that pops into your head. 'Attracts me like a cauliflower' is his idea for 'Something'.

After all the humour, incessant work, disputes, and the first mention of Allen Klein, they gave us a fabulous finale. The live session on the roof took place at the end of January 1969, and in February of that year they would cheerfully get down to work on the masterpiece that is *Abbey Road*.

From the point of view of the public, the rooftop gig was the last time we would see them perform as a live band. It was a collective decision to play on the roof, after many debates throughout January, but uncannily the ending of the concert was predicted in a discussion between Paul McCartney and Michael Lindsay-Hogg in early January. Paul says, 'It's almost in a way we [should] do the show in a place we're not allowed to do it. You know, like we should trespass, go in, set up and then get moved – and that should be the show. Getting forcibly ejected, still trying to play your numbers, and the police lifting you.'

Could there have been a better way to go, high above the city, almost floating, and with the police on their way? It was as positive as Paul wanted: this beautiful, poignant and fitting climax, the four of them, with the great Billy Preston on keyboards, on a gloomy day on a cramped and dangerous-looking roof in Savile Row, where the band can barely be seen by anyone. It took place in London too, interrupted by cops who look younger than the band.

Don't cry about it. The end of The Beatles was as necessary as it was inevitable, as important and liberating as the end of any relationship. The Sixties were done; the Seventies would be darker and The Beatles were only rarely a dark band. Something else, far harder and crueller, would be required. After *Abbey Road* there would be Bowie's *Hunky Dory*.

Bowing out is an art too. We are aware of the end even as we read these conversations. They discuss it openly, and with little rancour. Before he walked out and then came back, George said, 'I think we should have a divorce,' with Paul replying, 'Well, I said that at the last meeting. But it's getting near it, you know.'

Not long before the poignant finish on the roof there'd been a glimpse back, moving paeans to their dead mothers: McCartney's 'Let It Be', and Lennon's 'Julia'. Then the two songwriters left their childhoods behind, disappearing into the future, where they would concentrate on the important work of being parents. They'd been kids for a long time. But they can't, after all, even agree where or whether to play live at all. Their friendship remains, but their enthusiasm for one another has waned, as it would have to.

We weren't there with them, but The Beatles must have felt that they had become actors in someone else's play. They must have become tired of everyone staring at them all day. Unlike almost every other group, they retained the affection of the general public, and never lost it. But what a confinement it had become, and they knew it too. Significantly, the album which became known as 'The White Album' was, at one point, going to be called *A Doll's House* after Ibsen's play, at the end of which the heroine Nora flees into a new life, famously slamming the door behind her. Now The Beatles required new people to help them find out what sort of talent they had, apart from the others, as free singular individuals. That was important. And who can't agree that they needed time and space to figure out what exactly sort of fame hurricane they'd been through, a whirlwind like nothing seen before?

They had to escape. And we had to let them go. We owed them that, after what they'd done for us. The four of them would go on working, playing and entertaining us. It was their living, their life and destiny. Our tribute is to play the records, and hand them on to our kids, while thanking the band, and being grateful every time we hear those voices for some of the most beautiful pop songs ever created.

DRAMATIS PERSONAE

John Lennon

George Harrison

Paul McCartney

Ringo Starr

Michael Lindsay-Hogg
Director

Glyn Johns
Recording engineer

Tony Richmond
Cinematographer

Denis O'Dell
Head of Apple Films

Neil Aspinall
Managing Director, Apple

Mal Evans
Road Manager, Apple

Derek Taylor
Press officer, Apple

Kevin Harrington
Runner, Apple

George Martin
Producer

Billy Preston
Keyboard player

Yoko Ono
Artist

Ethan A. Russell
Photographer

Linda Eastman
Photographer

Heather
Daughter of Linda Eastman

Peter Sellers
Actor

Dick James
*Managing Director,
Northern Songs*

ACT ONE: TWICKENHAM FILM STUDIOS

2–16 JANUARY 1969

JOHN HARRIS

Only two and a half months after the end of sessions for the so-called 'White Album' and with Christmas barely over, The Beatles regroup to begin work on their new project. The fan magazine *The Beatles Book* has recently announced that they are about to start 'preparing the world's biggest concert… an hour-long show which will be seen on a hundred million television screens all around the world.' The director will be Michael Lindsay-Hogg, whose past work with the group includes promotional films for 'Paperback Writer' and 'Rain', and more recently 'Hey Jude' and 'Revolution'. Despite advance discussions about where and how to hold this event, no decisions have been reached. To keep the project moving forwards, it is agreed that rehearsals should take place at Twickenham Film Studios in West London, and be filmed.

George has spent several weeks in the USA, working with the Apple Records artist Jackie Lomax, and spending time in upstate New York with Bob Dylan and The Band. As well as being centrally involved in Apple's affairs and writing new songs, Paul has been immersed in his new relationship with Linda Eastman, spending time at his farm in Scotland and holidaying in Portugal. John has been dragged through the courts after being charged with cannabis possession, his new partner Yoko Ono has suffered a miscarriage and, as well as releasing an album titled *Two Virgins* and filming performances in *The Rolling Stones Rock And Roll Circus* (also directed by Lindsay-Hogg), the two of them have finished work on an avant-garde movie titled *Rape*. Ringo is preparing for his role alongside Peter Sellers in *The Magic Christian*, work on which will commence on 3 February.

The group's stay at Twickenham will see them working on new songs for what are initially conceived as two performances. Their thinking is that if the planned show(s) takes place, footage of these rehearsals and preparations could be used for a supporting TV show that will promote the main event: as Lindsay-Hogg will later put it, 'a 20-minute, [or] 30-minute documentary about the making of the television special, just to hype it'.

Having become accustomed to working from the late afternoon or evening into the small hours at Abbey Road, the four of them are suddenly required to begin well before lunch. The crew are to be on-set at 8.30am; The Beatles, in theory at least, are required to be there an hour and a half later. Paul regularly travels from his home in St John's Wood via public transport, and approaches work in a spirit of optimism. John and George, by contrast, will later recall these early sessions as a trial; as John sees it, 'You couldn't make music at eight in the morning, or ten or whatever it was, in a strange place with people filming you, and coloured lights.'

Though 18 January has been tentatively set as the date for a performance, as The Beatles start work the group and their associates are still unsure about where they are going to play, who exactly will form the watching crowd, or whether a show should take place at all. Discussions about these matters, usually in the company of Denis O'Dell, the head of Apple Films, are a daily feature of the Twickenham experience. Perhaps the most head-turning idea is a performance at the Roman amphitheatre in Sabratha, Libya – at one point conceived as the destination of a journey by ocean liner which will transport The Beatles, the film crew and a specially selected audience.

What happens at Twickenham over the following nine days is filmed using two cameras. There is no studio-quality recording equipment, but music and conversations are captured by two Nagra tape recorders, standard equipment for capturing film sound. So soon after the recording and release of their last album, The Beatles remain extraordinarily productive: the number of new songs and the easy, free-flowing conversations among four friends show that they are hardly locked into decline, but some disagreements begin to surface, sparked off by their surroundings and their diverging approaches to recording or playing live.

THURSDAY
2 JANUARY
1969

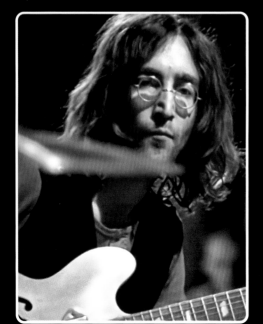

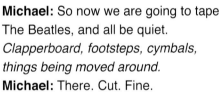

Michael: So now we are going to tape The Beatles, and all be quiet. *Clapperboard, footsteps, cymbals, things being moved around.*
Michael: There. Cut. Fine.

Enter Ringo, George, John and Yoko, and a solitary Hare Krishna devotee, who keeps his distance.
George: [comically] Hi Ringo.
Ringo: Hi George.
George: Happy New Year.
John: Hi Ringo, happy New Year.
Ringo: Happy New Year.

The three of them have an initial go at 'Dig A Pony'.
John: [to Ringo] Have you heard Eric Burdon's new one? It's pretty good.
Ringo: It's an old one, isn't it?

George shows the others 'All Things Must Pass'; John leads an early run-through of 'Don't Let Me Down'.
George: That's a good one. I like simple tunes.
John: Yeah, 'Ring Of Fire'. [laughs].

Ringo: Yeah, that's right – Johnny Cash.
John: His voice sounds great on it… sounds like he's got back to 'House Of The Rising Sun'.

John plays 'Dig A Pony'. George plays 'Let It Down'. John then shows the others 'Child Of Nature' and 'Sun King'.

Enter Paul, followed by George Martin.
George: Happy New Year.
Paul: Same to you.
Paul: [to John] What key are you in? E?
John: E.
Paul: Tune up?
George: Or down, maybe we're wrong.
Paul: I don't know – I'll come with you.
John: No, I think we're about constant.

Paul shows them an early version of 'I've Got A Feeling'.
John: I've got something to do at the end.
Paul: Yeah.
John: Makes it interesting.

A little later, George expresses concerns about the acoustics of the film studios.

Paul: [to Michael and George Martin] Nobody is sort of definitely struck on this place [i.e. Twickenham]. We'll have two weeks where we can play this and I'm thinking… you know, we all say, 'Right everybody out of here, and go into the hut' – and we'll just cram people into the hut and really have a Cavern [club] thing in a hut. And that'll be great, won't it?

They play 'I've Got A Feeling'.

George: Is that one called 'I've Got A Feeling'?

John: Well I've got a hard on!

Paul: Everybody had a hard on… [laughs]

John: [sings] 'Everybody had a hard on…'

Paul: 'Except for me and my monkey.' [laughs]

Enter Glyn Johns. Some time later, Paul, Michael, Glyn and Tony begin a long conversation.

Paul: This place sounds terrible now, but it may just be great, you never know.

Michael: Well this, the PA stuff is arriving this afternoon, isn't it?

Kevin: About half an hour.

Michael: Great.

Paul: You can never tell with these places, though.

Glyn: Yeah. No.

Paul: Supposed to be terrible acoustically, but we did a track in a little room like a bog, you know, and we were like, 'No separation in there,' you know, and we really got good separation. We did 'Yer Blues' in there.

Glyn: Yeah?

Michael: I think the thing to do is just to be very flexible about every aspect of the enterprise.

Laughing.

Paul: [camply] Michael, I think you are pretty right. Pretty fair comment.

They eventually talk further about the possibilities of the proposed live show.

Glyn: The thing is that an open-air sound is fantastic. I've always wanted to do something in the open air.

Michael: I was very taken by the place Denis talked about, the amphitheatre [in Sabratha, Libya]. Because the whole thing… I could see, torch-lit, two thousand Arabs, and friends around. And I thought the venue was appropriate.

Paul: I think you'll find we are not going abroad, 'cos Ringo just said he doesn't want to go abroad and he put his foot down. So, us and Jimmie Nicol might go abroad.

Jimmie Nicol had been the stand-in drummer for several Beatles concerts overseas in 1964 when Ringo had tonsillitis.

Michael: I think the thing to do is just see what we all feel in a day or two as opposed to making anything hard and fast immediately. 'Cos we may find the

idea – or any idea – grows and gets more attractive or less attractive given where you are now.

Paul: It would be nice to try and find some way to do it out of doors.

Glyn: But it's so bloody cold, isn't it? That's the thing.

Michael: It's your English rain which is worrying about out of doors in this country.

Paul: I wouldn't mind playing in the rain…

Glyn: That would be interesting.

Paul: Snow or rain would do me, you know. It's just the frozen hands trying to play those notes…

Glyn: Trying to get your E-7th when your little finger's frozen…

Paul: It's all right. [archly] You might just have a few deaths on the set due to electric shocks.

Michael: I just thought if it's raining it's just not all that fun, if you're going to do it for two or three days. I mean, if we did it at the end of the month in Slough out in the fields, in the audience we'd have

eight pigs and seven farmers… I think the thing is to be flexible, he said finally.

The band continue to work on 'I've Got A Feeling' and 'Don't Let Me Down'.

George: Any buns or anything?

John: Yeah there's some, there's some in the bag under here. George?

George: Do you want some sandwiches? Paul, do you want some sandwiches? Hang on… [whistles to Ray Freeborn, assistant director]

John: Ray, do you want a dry bun?

George: Oh, don't eat that.

John: I mean it's nice but it's…

George: A dry bun, yeah.

John: It's like a rock cake, but it needs butter or something.

Yoko: These are vegetarian if you want some, George.

Ringo: Some rolls and things.

George: [eating] Mmm, that's what I want. You know – anything.

Work begins on 'Two Of Us'. The day's shooting comes to a close.

FRIDAY
3 JANUARY
1969

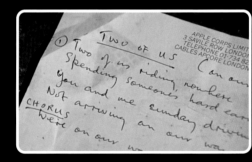

Paul and Ringo are the first to arrive. At the piano, Paul plays a snatch of 'The Long And Winding Road' (without vocals), then 'Oh! Darling' and 'Maxwell's Silver Hammer', Samuel Barber's Adagio for Strings *and Vincent Youmans and Irving Caesar's 'Tea For Two', followed by an early version of 'Let It Be'. Enter George, who has a copy of the fan magazine* The Beatles Book.

Ringo: Hi George.
George: Sorry for being late but I fell asleep again.
Paul: John's late [laughs].
George: *Beatles Book*.
Paul: Good this month?
George: Seems to be getting older and older.
Paul: Deteriorating.

Ringo: Slipping back into its old ways.
George: Yep. And it seems to be a good thing.
At the piano, Ringo plays a self-penned work in progress titled 'Taking A Trip To Carolina'.
Ringo: [sings] 'Taking a trip on an ocean liner/ I got a girl from Carolina/ Taking a trip on an ocean liner/ I've gotta get to Carolina/ Even though it's gonna get harder for me… Taking a trip on an ocean liner/ I gotta get to Carolina/ Taking a trip on an ocean liner/ Hmmmm…'
George: [looking at photograph in magazine] What do you think of George's pseudo-tie sweatshirt? I think it's terrible.
Laughing.

Mal: Do you want tea, or anything?
George: Er, I'll have a cup of tea, yeah. Thanks Mal. [reading] 'The true story of The Beatles. If you have not been able to obtain it, you can still get it direct.'
Paul: [sings] Ooooooo…
George: [reading] 'Accompanied by his current steady, American photographer Linda Eastman, Paul spent a December week in Portugal visiting The Beatles' biographer, Hunter Davies.'
Mal: Do you want tea, or anything?
George: [singing, with acoustic guitar] 'Now don't crowd me, lady, or I'll fill up your shoes/ I'm a sweet bourbon daddy, and tonight I'm blue… Please, Mrs Henry, Mrs Henry, please/ Mrs Henry, Mrs Henry, please/ I'm down on my knees/ And I ain't got a dime…'
Ringo: Been listening to some blues?
George: Did you play those tapes of Dylan's?
Ringo: Oh yeah, I played… no, only the one I played.
George: Really? They're great… The Band, you know, are too much. They're just happy to be a band. The drummer is fantastic 'cos he plays guitar really; he's not really the drummer, you know. Levon Helm, he's called… their favourite track [on 'The White Album'] was Ringo's track ['Don't Pass Me By']… You know, that's their scene completely.
Paul: Yeah, great. [To Ringo] Are you going to write another?
Ringo huffs.
Paul: Yeah, okay. I know, I understand.
Ringo: Yes I am, but you know it's just…
Paul: I know, I realise it's a daft question.
Ringo: I really do get fed up with…
Paul: Not knowing the chords yet?
Ringo: [plays piano chords] How do you do it?
George: Oh, what's that one? He's [i.e. Ringo's] got a great one…
Paul: 'Picasso'?
George: Yeah.
Ringo: Yeah, but I can't fit it in when I play it, that's the only drag with that.
Paul: Let's hear it, 'cos actually it's a fast one too, isn't it?

Ringo: [laughs] It's too fast for me. [sings] 'I bought a Picasso… I bought a Picasso [laughs]/ Looked at it upside down, then the other way/ I couldn't find a lady nowhere/ To me it looked like a wooden chair.' See, then I need to do something.
Paul: [sings] 'Oh baby.'
Ringo: [sings, affirmatively] 'Oh baby.'
Paul: You should do it though, yeah.
Ringo: Yeah, and I've got 'Taking A Trip To Carolina'.

Ringo plays 'Taking A Trip To Carolina'.
Ringo: I've got it on the little tape, singing that I've been to LA and New York too, so they're not very nice, you know – the words mean they're not good. But Carolina – it's my baby.
Paul: Okay. Just get me back there.

A few moments later…
George: I've been thinking of all the tunes I've got, and they're all slowish.
Paul: Yeah, most of mine are.
George: I've got that Taxman Part Two.
Paul: Oh yeah.
George: Taxman Revisited.
Paul: Yeah. '5-Year Slog'.
George: It's long. But it should be, like, [a] very sad type, you know, with maybe a string or two.
Paul: [approvingly] Mmm-mmm.
George: See, so far there's a couple that I know I could do live with no backing and that was one of them, that one… [plays, and sings, jokingly] 'When you're smiling…'
Paul: Oh yeah, just with no backing. Just with a guitar and singing.
George: Well, you know, that's how I've been doing it and that's how it sounded all the time. But it'd probably be nicer to do it…
Paul: If you can do that, that'd be great.
Ringo: Mmm… It'd be great.

George briefly plays 'All Things Must Pass' with Paul on drums. Enter John and Yoko. With Paul still on drums, John and Paul play 'Don't Let Me Down'. With Ringo back in place, the band then play the Elvis hit

'All Shook Up', Carl Perkins's 'Your True Love' and 'Blue Suede Shoes', The Coasters' B-side and early Beatles staple 'Three Cool Cats', Bob Dylan's 'Blowin' In The Wind', and Little Richard's 'Lucille'. They then play jokey renditions of 'I'm So Tired' – sung by Paul – and 'Ob-La-Di, Ob-La-Da'.

Paul/John: [singing] 'Desmond has a barrow in the marketplace/ Doris had another in the bog!/ Charlie had another at his black hotel/ And Lordy! Lordy! Did they have a bag of fun!… Oh my God! Oh my God! Oh my God…'
John: 'Desmond has his sparrow in his pocket book/ Molly had an eagle in the Strand/ Molly said to Desi, "Boy, I like your hook, and when you hit me I believe you're in the band!"'
George: 'La, la life goes on/ La, la, la, la, la, life goes on…'

They then run through 'One After 909'.
Paul: Okay.
George: That went all right.
Paul: Yeah.
George: [enthusiastically] We should do it.
John: I wrote that when I was about fifteen.
Paul: Incredible, isn't it?
John: I always meant to just change the words a bit, and do something better.
Paul: No! It's great: 'One after 909/ So move over honey, I'm travelling on that line…'
Laughing.
Paul: 'Move over once, move over twice, come on baby, don't be cold as ice…'
John/Paul: [sings] 'You're only fooling round, you're only fooling round with me…'
Paul: It's great. [laughs]
George: Yeah, well, shall we just practise that for a bit? Or maybe we should just do it without practising it.
John: What?
George: You know, practising will fuck it up.
Paul: I never sort of knew what it was about before.
John: No, I never [did].
Paul: I mean, so she's on a train.
John: Yes.
Paul: And he sort of…
John: He goes to the station and he misses it.
Laughing.
Paul: But he goes back and finds it was the wrong number, so…
George: Wrong location.
John: To rhyme with station, you know.
Paul: Our kid's [i.e Mike McCartney's] been saying you should do that for years, you know.
John: Yeah, he always liked that, didn't he?
George: I've always liked it. You know, most people just don't give a shit what the words are about. [laughs]
Paul: Yeah, right.

George: As long as it's, you know, just popping along.
Paul: Yeah.

John and Paul remind themselves of other early Lennon-McCartney songs: 'I'll Wait Till Tomorrow', 'I've Been Thinking That You Love Me', 'Won't You Please Say Goodbye'. The band move on to Sam Cooke's 'Bring It On Home To Me', Marvin Gaye's 'Hitch Hike' and 'You Can't Do That', followed by Chan Romero's 'The Hippy Hippy Shake'. They then work on 'Two Of Us', and a new song written by John that will be titled 'Gimme Some Truth', before determinedly turning to 'All Things Must Pass'.
George: Are we not going to do any 'oldies but goldies' on this show?
Paul: Don't know. We could do.
Michael: I do think it would be nice.
George: It would, you know. And also from the *selling* point of view… In America, you know, I was saying…
Paul: [to Michael] Give us a cigar, then.
Paul is handed a cigar, and starts smoking it.
George: Just to hit the first initial thing of us singing all completely new ones: they need something to identify with… So, it would be nice to just start the show, or end the show, with a couple of…
John: We'll rock some up like Joe Cocker did. I've been doing 'Help!' pretty good so…
Yoko: Yeah, 'Help!' is nice.
George: I tell you which is a good one… er…

He and Paul play and sing 'Every Little Thing', from Beatles For Sale.
Michael: You want one of those rock'n'roll songs. I mean, like 'Good Golly Miss Molly'.
Paul: Oh, those, those kind of songs? Yeah, well, we'll do it.
Michael: 'Cos you are a great rock'n'roll group.

After 'All Things Must Pass', the band work on 'Maxwell's Silver Hammer'. George says the availability of recording equipment in America is much better than in the UK. There is mention of 'Magic' Alex Mardas, the head of Apple Electronics, working on new kit in Boston Place, Marylebone.

Michael: See you Monday at ten, right?
Paul: Yeah. Ta-ra!
John: Ta-ra! See you, er, yeah. See you Monday, yeah.
Michael: So long. See you Monday. Have a nice W-E-E-K-E-N-D!

MONDAY
6 JANUARY
1969

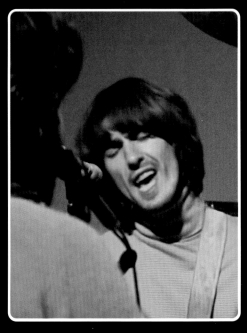

  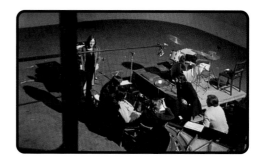

Paul is the first to arrive. With Michael Lindsay-Hogg and Glyn Johns, he discusses Cream drummer Ginger Baker and also Barry Ryan's hit 'Eloise', before they talk about work done the previous week.

Paul: The one I'm most pleased about is 'One After 909'.
Michael: What's that one?
Paul: Just the one we were doing the other day – 'One After 909'.
Glyn: Oh yeah, that was fantastic.
Paul: That's great.
Glyn: Really great.
Michael: Which one?
Paul: You know, one of the first songs we'd ever done.
Glyn: Right. It was John who wrote it when he was fifteen or something…
Paul: It's just we all used to sag off every school day, and go back to my house, and the two of us would just sort of sit there and write 'Love Me Do', and 'Too Bad About Sorrows'. And there's a lot from then, you know. There's about a hundred songs from then that we've never reckoned 'cos they were all very unsophisticated songs. You know [sings]: 'They said our love was just fun/ The day that our friendship begun… There's no blue moon that I can see/ There's never been in history…' But, you know, they're great. And that one, we always hated the words: [speaks/ sings] 'My baby says she's travelling on the one after 909/ I said move over honey I'm travelling on that line [giggles]/ I said move over once, move over twice/ Come on baby don't be cold as ice…' [laughs] But they're great.
Michael: Oh, they're great songs.
Glyn: I called it 'Move Over' in my book [laughs], in me notes.

Enter Ringo.
Paul: Good morning.
Ringo: Arrrghhhhh…
Paul: Good mornink! Ooh!
Ringo: I won't lie. I'm not too good.
Glyn: Join the club.

Enter John and Yoko.
Michael: How are you?
Paul: Hiya. [laughs] Good morning.
Yoko laughs.
John: The night is love.
Michael: We ought to think this week sometime about the show.
Paul: But we *are* thinking about the show, Michael.
John: We never stop thinking about it.
Paul: What you mean is *you* ought to think about the show.
Michael: We can do it at the Albert Hall…

Enter George.
Paul: Morning, George.
George: Morning, all.
Ringo: Morning, George.
George: Didn't have any sleep last night.
John: Didn't you? Why?
Paul: Just through lack of sleep?
George: Just through… because we're getting… it gets a bit late. You know, it just gets so late that it's early.
Paul: Yeah.
George: And then you're just, you know, dropping off and it's still dark, and it's Mal [Evans] calling, and all that.
Michael: There also comes a point where it's not worth sleeping, I think.
Laughing.
George: Oh, it's fun, though. I feel quite

good, actually. [To Paul] I was trying to ring you this morning.
Paul: Yes, I know.
George: To wake you up.
Paul: I know. I was complaining to the operator, and telling him: 'Can I tell you about my phone going wrong?' But I hadn't switched it through.
Michael: Wouldn't it be nice if we did this show with a big audience?
Paul: Yes.
George: I think we should forget the whole idea of this show.
[smiles]
Laughing.
Paul: Yeah. Just, that's it. Okay. I'll go along with that. We're back to square one.
Michael: Square one. I like that. I like being flexible. I think that's important.
Paul moves to the organ.
Paul: I had a bit the other night which might interest you. It was while I was thinking of a song for Ringo, which went [sings], 'Boy, you're gonna carry that weight, carry that weight a long time/ Boy, you're gonna carry that weight, carry that weight a long time…'
All together now…
All: [singing] 'Boy, you're gonna carry that weight, carry that weight a long time/ Boy, you're gonna carry that weight, carry that weight a long time…'

The band move on to 'Across The Universe', 'I've Got A Feeling', 'Don't Let Me Down' and 'One After 909', before George plays 'Hear Me Lord' to John and Paul.

Paul: Is this the new song?

George: It's not particularly for this.

Paul: It'll be in the show.

George: It's great to just get great ideas. They just get me like The Staple Singers, you know, as part of the show… just, you know, really groovy singers.

Enter Denis O'Dell from Apple Films, Neil Aspinall and George Martin. A long conversation starts about plans for the show.

Michael: Any stage performance now of an ordinary sort, visually, will never be topped, because we all remember – I mean, you better than I…

Paul: Okay. So what's the use of an audience?

Yoko: Right, right.

Paul: The use of an audience is like for you, out of sheer charity, to play to them because you love 'em? Or for you to collect ticket money? Or to get a reaction between you for the sake of your show?

Michael: Yes.

Paul: But look, the thing is, then, that's presuming that *we're* not enough for a show.

Yoko: Yeah, so that's very bad, you know.

Paul: That does presuppose that there's not enough in the four of us, [so] you've really got to pan off onto a postman.

Paul is referring to the moment in the 'Hey Jude' promo when the camera pans to a postman.

George Martin: No, not so, Paul.

Denis: Yes, you see, the point…

George Martin: The whole point about an audience, surely, is to give you something when you're performing.

George: It's good and bad, really.

George Martin: It's to give you a reaction.

George: Yeah, I suppose.

Michael: Yeah, like a, like an actor on stage.

George: To bounce back, yeah.

Michael: It's a different audience, a live audience.

George: Well, it'd just be our luck to get a lot of cunts in there.

Michael: But equally, once you get on a stage, you are performers, and you've got to have someone to do it to – either the camera or real people, I think.

Yoko: Well, empty chairs could be much more dramatic. I mean, twenty thousand empty chairs is much more dramatic.

George: Or we could have some cardboard cut-outs.

Michael: Looks like they haven't bought any tickets! [laughs]

Paul: Yes. But the thing is, no one's going to think that, Mike. Nobody's going to think that they haven't bought any tickets, you know. It'll just be: 'They've done it to twenty thousand live chairs.' [laughs]

Yoko: [forcefully] And also, you know, people are wondering what kind of audience you have now, you know. And it should be like The Invisible Nameless Everybody In The World, you know, instead of some teenager or something… Or if you have costumed people they say, 'Oh, those are the audience now.' It's very dangerous, you know…

Paul: Mmm-hmm.

Yoko: So…

George: Oh, it'd be great to have two thousand chairs but with the audience…

Denis: But it's like that small bandstand in Hyde Park: that Regency bandstand, empty! It stands there every week and it's super, that empty bandstand, you know… it's knockout, that whole thing. Empty. Empty.

Michael: I think it's a very good idea. That's sounds to me more, though, like five minutes rather than fifty minutes. What we *want* to attack is all over the world. I mean, it oughtn't to be the kids who queue up outside the gate. It really ought to be the whole world.

Denis: Yeah.

Yoko: Yeah.

Michael: And that was one of the things we tried to get on '[Hey] Jude': everybody.

Paul: Hey look, we're doing two shows, aren't we?

Michael: Yes.

Paul: We're taping the shows on the Sunday and the Monday, or something… It splits the idea a bit. It means that we're going to do half of two ideas.

Michael: I think it'll be better if in the end we arrive at one idea.

Paul: You know, I like the idea of just theoretically doing one idea.

Denis: One idea, one idea.

Yoko: Yep, right.

Paul: But we are doing two shows. And the idea could be to play one night to silence, and the next night to those chairs filled.

Denis: Yeah. It'd be sort of nice…

Yoko: But the people who are watching the TV don't want to see an audience, unless the audience is terribly different, you know, like…

Paul: That's what I mean.

Michael: I think the audience *could* be different.

Yoko: Everybody's completely formal… you know, queens and kings coming to see it.

George Martin: I think that if you get rid of an audience then there's no point in doing a live performance. It's like going into a recording studio and doing one take.

Michael: But I think we think we should have a different kind of audience.

Denis: Well, unless it's because of the backgrounds, George, you see. Unless we're going right back to Sabratha, you see.

Glyn: I also think that an audience being used visually in the show isn't a bad thing, because I think people are very interested in seeing how an audience would react to you, although they've seen it before.

Yoko: You have to announce in the newspaper saying that it's going to

be a real live show for, you know, The Beatles. And then I think it'll be a crazy scene like everybody queuing for it, and everything…

Denis: Is what you're saying, [that] it should be an Albert Hall scene?

Yoko: Yeah, right. Then it should be the Albert Hall.

Denis: Exactly. I feel that too.

Michael: Yes. I'm not against Albert Hall. I just think that it slightly smells of a few years ago.

Yoko: All right, say anything and it will slightly smell like either a few years ago or less than a few years ago.

Michael Exactly. Unless it was a *location*. [Sabratha] is a location, which is marvellous in itself, by the sea, with a…

Paul: [definitively] Mmm. But look – that has to be in England. An outdoor scene has to be in England.

Denis: It's going to be very cold.

Paul: We've decided we're not going abroad.

Denis: I don't think it's practical to do it in England, it's too bloody cold.

Paul: Right, that's what I think.

Glyn: Yeah.

Paul: But we have decided that there's a definite decision that we're not going abroad, so we should sort of rule that out.

Denis: It would be literally in your back garden.

Michael: Your back garden looks like a little promotional film to me, as opposed to a Beatles television show.

Paul: [laughs] You need a house! Let's do it in my place.

Sound of background chatter.

Paul: See I think the thing is, though… Okay, so we were prepared to do it with an audience. But what Yoko says is right, you know, that we can't just have the same old audience…

Michael: She's totally right.

Paul: … or the same old scene. It's not even the same old scene. If it was the same old audience and we were all naked when they came in, then that'd be a different scene, you know.

Michael: Mmm. I think she's totally right about that. I mean, that's one of my big points.

Paul: So no, we shouldn't really try to do anything with the audience because the audience is the audience, you know. It's us that's doing the show.

George: Maybe just the audience should all be starkers!

Paul: But you'd never get that together, you know. That'd be like a half-arsed idea.

Michael: Or totally assed!

Denis: It would be nice, though, wouldn't it?… Perhaps we should do it to a different sort of audience. Perhaps we should do it in the Royal Academy, or the Tate Gallery, with nobody there except the pictures?

Yoko: That makes much more sense, I think.

Denis: With nobody there except the pictures.

Michael: But I think once you get up to perform as The Beatles, you've got to be performing to *someone*, even if it's going to be this different kind of audience because…

Denis: Suppose you don't use human beings as [the] audience, what do you replace them with apart from animals? [laughs]

Paul: Dogs?

Michael: Men from the moon. You could do men from the moon.

Neil: Michael, you've got to remember that the audience that they're doing it for is sitting at home watching television… that's the audience, don't forget.

Yoko: Right, right, exactly.

Michael: If you just get up to perform, you've either got to be performing directly to the people at home, or to an audience.

Denis: Yeah.

Michael: I think there's only two ways… We *have* to think about the audience because you are so riddled with audience. I mean, the audience is so much part of the first half of you, musically. You know what I mean? The audience is so much part of the whole mystique.

The band work on the arrangement of 'Don't Let Me Down'.

George: Erm, what's the date today, by the way? Do you know?

Paul: Sixth.

Michael: Is today the sixth? I think so.

George: And what day is the…

Paul: Twelve days. Off.

John: What is off?

Paul: There's twelve days off is when we do it [i.e. the show].

Some time later, after more work on 'Don't Let Me Down'…

Paul: Okay… we haven't done many [songs] yet.

George: We've only fucking run through about four. We haven't really learnt any at all.

Paul: No, no.

They continue working on the song.

Paul: So that's near enough for the time being. I think we'll get it…

John: You've still got that hole, it's like the beat's still wrong.

George: No, really…

Paul: Yeah. Well, we've got to improve on that.

George: If we had a tape recorder now and just taped that and played it back, you'd throw that out straight away.

The band move on to 'Two Of Us'.
Paul: Okay, now…
John: What? Am I singing on this, or what?
Paul: I don't know, really. Melody. [sings] 'Two of us'… You have to remember the words too.
John: Yes, I've got 'em here.
Paul: But learn 'em.
John: Yes. I almost know them.
Work on the song continues.
Paul: It slows down there. Something sort of happens. But just don't… ignore it, you know. Just let it. [sings] 'You and I have memories… you and I have memories…'
George: How do you mean it slows down?
Paul: I mean ignore the fact that it changes into a middle eight.
George: I see. I thought you meant we must slow down.
Paul: No, no.
George: It's a long break, that one. [sings] 'Going home/ You and I have memories…'
Paul: 1, 2, 3, 4…
The song resumes.
Paul: See, like, we're really, we're going to have to bring it together 'cos we're all at odds. We're doing that thing we did on *The Beatles* [i.e 'The White Album']. We're all playing, you know… Do you know what I mean? We've got to get…

George: Yeah, but that's…
Paul: … the riffs, when the riffs bits [*sic*] come there.
George: There's no riffs. I mean, it's nice just to get what you play.
Paul: No, but it's… look, you and I aren't in…
George: [sings] 'You and I are memories… longer than the road…'
Paul: It's not together so that it's not *sounding* together even on…
George: … and so we can only play until we find the bit.
Paul: … or we can stop and say it's not together.
George: Yes, then you've got to carry on until it gets together, so, I mean, that's all right. I need to play until it sounds as though it's blending with the rest.
Paul: I never know what to say to that, you know, 'cos what I want to say is, 'Come on and play,' you know. But I can't… and then we get into that one.
George: Yes, because, er…
Paul: Okay! [sniggers] So here we go. *Bass.*
Paul: It's like it's complicated now. See, if we can get it simpler and then complicate it where it needs complications. But it's complicated in the bit…
George: It's not *complicated*. I'm just trying to… I mean, I'll play just the chords if you like, and then…

Paul: [quietly, with urgency] No, no, come on. You always get annoyed when I say that.

George: All I'm trying to do, I'm trying to find…

Paul: I'm trying to help, you know. But I always hear myself annoying you and I'm trying to…

George: No, you're not annoying me.

Paul: I get so I can't say…

George: You don't annoy me any more.

Paul: But you know what I mean? Well, you know, we do this then… and then, I don't know. Yeah, I can't do it on film either. [laughs] Can't fucking do it on camera…

John: Forget about candid camera.

Paul: I can't, though. You know, it's like I always sound like… I always feel as though I'm trying to put you down and stuff. But I'm not. I'm trying to stop us all playing until we know what we're playing.

George: Yeah, but you've got to play in order to find which fits and which doesn't… I mean, I'll wait until you get all your bits and then work my part out, if you like.

Paul: Yeah. I know.

George: Well, you know it's like that. It's like a matter of working it out with you while you're working your bit out. You know, have you got your bass bit?

Paul: Okay. Look, I'm not trying to say that. You know you're doing it again, as though I'm trying to say that. And what we said the other day, you know… I'm not trying to get you. I really am trying to just say, 'Look, lads, the band, you know, shall we… try it like this, you know?'

George: It's funny that it only occurs when we… the, erm…

Paul: I know it, it's this one. It's like,

'Shall we play guitar all though "Hey Jude"?' 'Well, I don't think we should.'

George: [animatedly] Yeah, okay, well I don't mind. I'll play, you know, whatever you want me to play, or I won't play at all if you don't want me to play. You know, whatever it is that'll please you, I'll do it. But I don't think you really know what that one is.

Paul: No. It's not like that now… Now we're rehearsing and we're trying to get it together for the TV show so we really… like you said, we've only been through four numbers.

George: Mmm-mmm. Well…

Paul: So we've probably got to get some system to get through like twenty or thirty and know 'em all and learn 'em all, and it's probably going to be like sculpture. So that we get all the chords, so we can all vamp 'em.

A few moments later.

Paul: You see, look, now this is the nub, I think. I think we've wasted a lot of time. I think we do, like, waste – physically waste – a hell of a lot of time, you know. And the four of us together…

John: I think if it's your song, you've got to do it exactly how you want it. You say, 'Don't play that. Play that.' It's up to you, you know…

Paul: But I'm scared of that one… me being the boss. And I have been for, like, a couple of years – and we all have, you know, no pretending about that… The problem is that we should all have written our own tunes – and if you want, like, improvisation then we should all say, 'Right… we improvise here.' But that would have… that puts much more work on each one of us then 'cos then we've got to work out my bass line.

John: I'd say improvise it, man.

Paul: [laughs] Yeah. But it's like a point of theory this, isn't it? You know, it's not just to do with playing music, this.

The day concludes with more run-throughs of 'All Things Must Pass'. Paul introduces the other three to 'She Came In Through The Bathroom Window'.

Paul: That'll do. Shall we go home?

John: Yes, all right.

Paul: Good night.

Ringo: Good night.

Paul: [sings] 'You're gonna carry that weight/ Carry that weight a long time/ Chucka-cha-cha/ Boy, you're gonna carry that…'

John: We were here a day, weren't we? See you tomorrow. Open-minded.

Michael: Open-minded, but keep flexible. See ya, kids. See you tomorrow. Ten, ten.

Paul: Ten, ten.

TUESDAY
7 JANUARY
1969

For the first time, Paul plays 'The Long And Winding Road' with vocals, followed by 'Golden Slumbers', which segues into 'Carry That Weight'. As George eats toast, he and Ringo sit on the drum riser.

George: [of Michael Lindsay-Hogg] His cigar doesn't half stink, doesn't it?
Ringo: Mmm.
George: Is Joe the chauffeur coming?
Mal: He comes up at lunchtime, around lunchtime.
George: Oh.
Mal: Do you want anything doing before then?
George: Yeah, well tell him to go out to our house before lunchtime.
Mal: Yeah, okay.
George: Why does he come at lunchtime?
Mal: He brings macrobiotics for John and Yoko.
George: Yesterday Paul was saying something about the picture of us all with Maharishi. Did you hear him say that?

Ringo: Mmm.
George: I was just messing around, and I saw a big colour picture, and I just looked at it, and it's too much.
Ringo: I'll have a look at it.
George: [laughs] You look all right.
Ringo: The one where we're all sitting round?
George: Oh, it's got Paul and Jane [Asher], and John and Cyn are on the right, and then there's Pattie and me, [and] you and Jenny [Boyd], I think.
Ringo: Yeah.
George: [laughs] And they just don't have a clue what it is they're sitting there holding the flowers for. It's too much. 'Cos I never thought about it, until I looked at it. Especially Paul and Jane and Cyn: they just looked in agony. And he was smiling.
Ringo: Who? Mahi?
George: Yeah. [laughs]
Paul: Lennon's late again.
Ringo: Well, between ten and eleven is the time.
Michael: No. One shouldn't be late...

Paul: I'm thinking of getting rid of him.
Ringo: I'm never late.
Michael: 'Cos everybody else is late once.
Paul: He's never late, he's a bloody pro is Ringo.

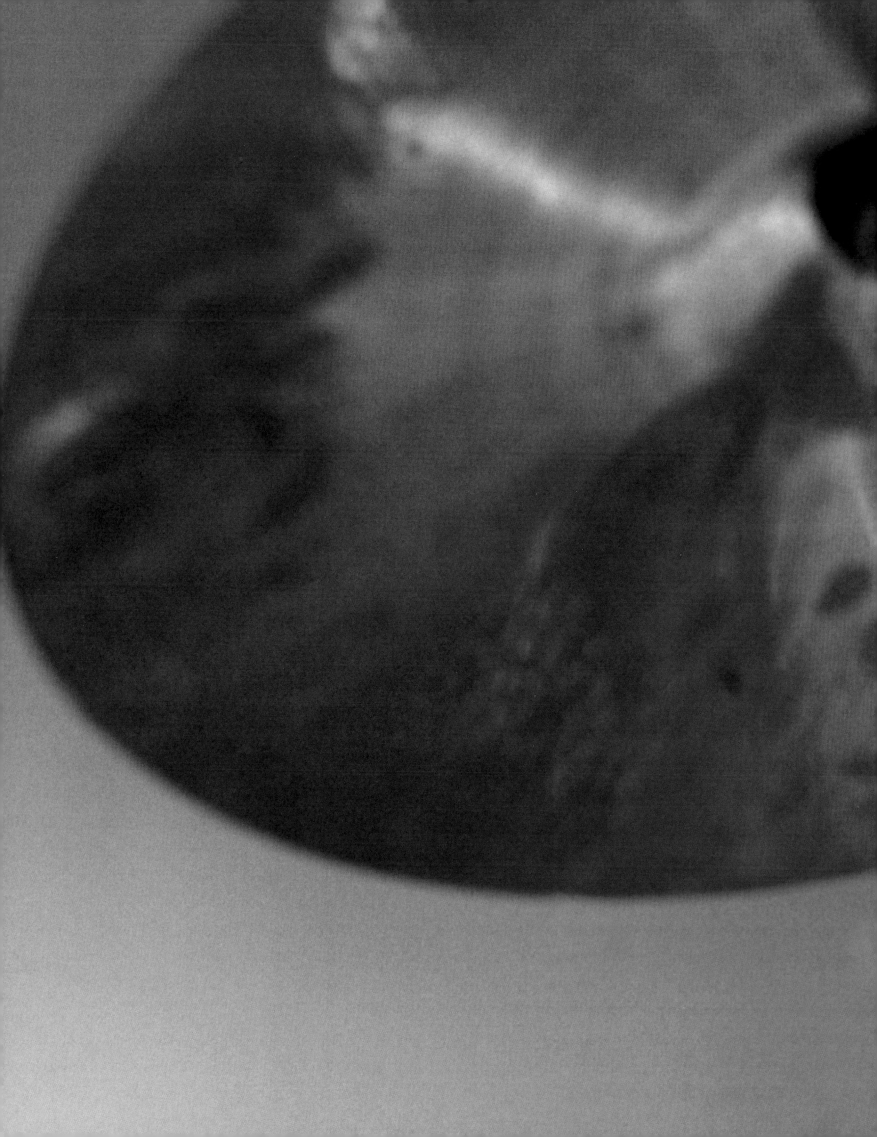

Enter John and Yoko. Paul leads a very early version of 'Get Back'. The words are mostly unfinished, but the verses and chorus are clearly taking shape. Ringo claps along. Some time later, as the band sit in a circle with their instruments…

Paul: If we cancel the show now we'd still be throwing it away… but that's the way we tend to do it: get halfway through a thing…

George: … and call it a day.

Paul: That's where all the money goes.

Michael: But I think that the worst we should have is a documentary. Which is a commercial enterprise. There's no reason, I think, why we shouldn't also get a show… Although none of us yet are happy with anything you've done in here.

Paul: I am.

Michael: Yeah, I don't… I don't agree with you.

Paul: It's fine. Come on – it's fine, you know. It's all right. The thing is, it's just not as good as it could be yet, but you know, here we are, we'll do it. We'll sing songs, you know. I mean, really, what you mean is that you haven't thought of the great idea yet. The great idea is leave us to it; just don't do the show.

George: That's pretty good.

John: If we can't think of any sort of gimmick, well, we just have… the worst that we have is a documentary of us making an LP, you know. If we don't get into a show.

Paul: Mmm.

John: Just make an LP.

George: Ever since Mr Epstein passed away…

John: Who passed away?

George: … it's never been the same.

Paul: No, because nobody'll take any… you won't ever say anything. It's going to be sort of dull. We've been very negative since Mr Epstein passed away. I mean, you know, that's why all of us in turn has been sick of the group, you know, 'cos there's nothing positive in it. You know,

it is a bit of a drag. But the only way for it not to be a bit of a drag is for the four of us to think, should we make it positive?

George: Well…

Paul: Or should we fuck it, you know? There's only two alternatives in it.

John: I've got an incentive. I've decided, all the things that we do… the whole point of it is communication.

Paul: Yeah.

John: And to be on TV is communication, 'cos we've got a chance to smile at people, like [the global broadcast of] 'All You Need Is Love'. So that's my incentive for doing it.

Michael: They both, 'All You Need Is Love' and 'Hey Jude', *did* communicate.

Paul: 'Course they did. 'Course they did.

John: Yeah, I just thought, you know, if we need to think of any incentive, the incentive is to communicate.

Michael: I agree.

Paul: There really is no one there now to say, 'Do that.' Whereas there always used to be. And we just sort of [think], 'Oh fucking hell, you know. Keep getting us up at eight?' But it's *us* that has to get us up at eight now, you know. But that's only growing up. You know, your daddy goes away at a certain point in your life. You stand on your own feet. I mean that's all we've been faced with – Daddy's gone away now, you know, and we're on our own at the holiday camp. And, you know, I think we either go home, or we do it.

Michael: I think if we've embarked on the enterprise, which is your decision… after all, you're all here… I think we ought to get as much as we can out of it because…

Paul: But any other director in the world would say, 'Fuck off!' you know. 'Fucking get off my set, you cunt!' You know, wouldn't they? If suddenly in the middle of a thing I was doing trying to pull together, four people just sort of shout, 'I don't think we want to do it!', you'd go, 'Oh fuck off." Anybody… I couldn't operate with that.

Michael: It's true.

Paul then focuses the conversation on the question of performing in front of an audience.

Paul: … You used to do it, lads. But we had a lot more incentive then.

George: [plays and sings] 'Ah, but I was so much older then/ I'm younger than that now.'

Paul: But we did. I mean, those films you're loving of us – that was us doing it, you know.

George: Well, if that's what doing it is, that's why I don't want to do it any more.

Paul: Yeah right. I think…

George: 'Cos I never liked that, and it was always your thang.

Paul: But you see nowadays you've grown up, and you don't have to do that any more. You see this is it. We don't have to put the pancake on, and go out in front, and sweat, and shake our heads [shakes head], 'cos we're not that any more. We've grown up a bit.

George: And because we've done that anyway.

Paul: Yeah, right. So… what I mean is that we did it then, but it doesn't mean [that] to do it again we have to do all that.

Michael: Right.

Paul: But now, for him [gestures towards John] to do it, it's to do a thing in a black bag with Yoko, you know…

This is a reference to John and Yoko's appearance in a large white bag at the Albert Hall in December 1968, at an alternative celebration of Christmas.

George: White bag.

Michael: White bag.

Paul: White bag. But that's it. You're doing it then on this level, you know.

Michael: But do you still want to perform in front of an audience, or do you just see yourselves as a recording group? I think it's communication, and I think part of communication is people seeing you doing it.

Paul: I think there's something to do with an audience there, yeah. I think we've got a bit shy, you know. I think I've got a bit shy of certain things, you know…

Michael: I guess maybe the difficulty is also getting up in front of an audience… trying to get something as good but maybe not the same thing. And that's a very hard thing to get back. In other words, you mustn't think of getting back what you had. Because you don't want it.

Paul: No, that's what Yoko was saying the other day, you know. We mustn't try and get in the audience and get 'em wild and…

Michael: Okay, although maybe… they've grown up as well. I mean, everyone in this room has grown up.

Paul: Yeah.

John: Yeah, I'm not worried about the audience.

Paul: We've really got to do what we do, but with the same kind of… it's not even discipline, it's the same kind of desire to do it somehow.

Michael: It's a drive. Desire. Wanting to do it… You've got to find something that you just want to go out and do it.

George: … Really I don't want to do *any* of my songs on the show. 'Cos I know they'll just turn out shitty… because they'd come out like a compromise, whereas in a studio then we can work on 'em… [and] get it how you want 'em.

Paul: But look, George – last year you were telling me that 'You can do anything you want, Paul. Anything you desire you can do,' you know.

George: Yeah.

Paul: But these days, you're saying, before the show is finished and before we've done it… we're not going to be able to do it, you know. They're [i.e the songs are] going to come out a compromise. Now I don't think that. I really don't. I really think we're *very good*. And we can get it together if we think that we want to do these songs great. We can just do it great, you know. But thinking it's not going to come out great won't help.

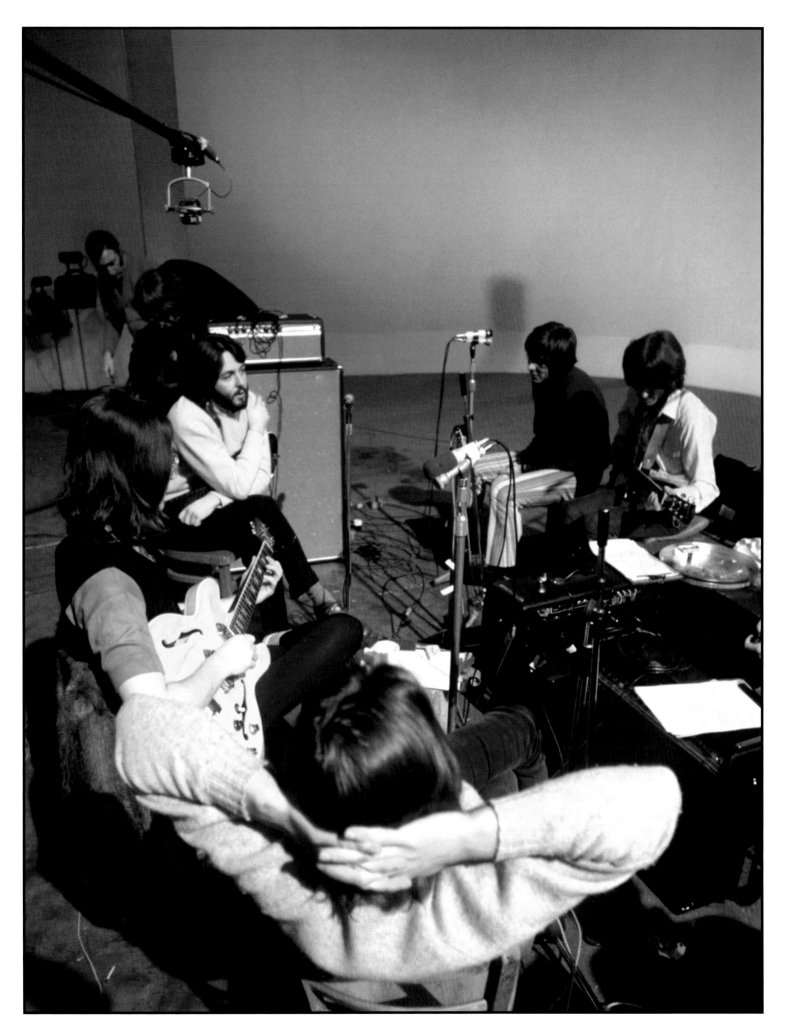

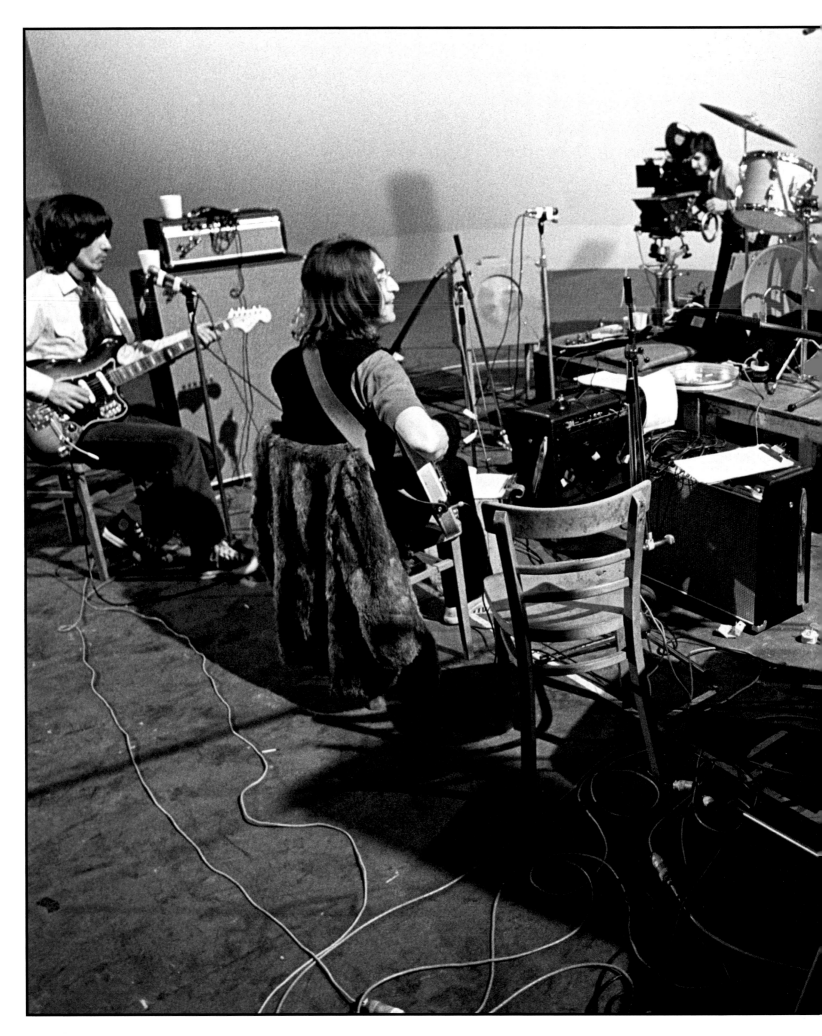

Some time later…
Paul: It's almost in a way we should do the show in a place we're not allowed to do it. You know, like we should trespass, go in, set up and then get moved – and that should be the show.
Michael: Yes.
Paul: Getting forcibly ejected, still trying to play your numbers, and the police lifting you.
Michael: I think that's too much of an obstacle!
Paul: With boots and truncheons, and all that, you know. You have to take a bit of violence.
Michael: I think that's too dangerous. I mean, that is an interesting thought: you all being beaten up. I mean, you could go back to Manila again.

Manila was the scene of The Beatles' terrifying 1966 encounter with a mob whipped up by Philippines President Ferdinand Marcos.
Paul: [laughs] Yeah.
George: Manila or Memphis.
Michael: Was Memphis bad? Well, Memphis is bad anyway.
Paul: Houston, as well.
George: Oh yeah. Texas.

In August 1966, The Beatles performed twice in Memphis, in the midst of the American controversy about John's 'more popular than Jesus' comments. They were picketed by the Ku Klux Klan, who had publicly threatened the group's safety. A year before, the group's arrival in Houston had been marked by fans climbing onto their plane and banging on the windows, before two shows in sweltering conditions where there were no dressing rooms.

George: Hear no evil. Speak no evil. See no evil!

Paul: I don't see why any of you – talking to whoever it is who's not interested – get yourselves into this, then. What's it for, you know? Can't be for the money! I mean, why are you here? I'm here 'cos, you know, I want to do a show. But I really don't feel an awful lot of support, you know. I mean, is anyone here 'cos they want to do a show [laughs]?

Michael: No, no. I mean, like Mal is right. Entertainment is almost enough; it's just where to put the entertainment…

Mal: Whatever the situation, the end result is… you play.

Paul: Yeah, but, I mean, you know, I'd do it, I'd do it in, er, suits on a stage show. I'd like to do a tour, you know, and all that.

A few moments later…

John: I said what I've been thinking.

Paul: Are you still thinking that now?

What are you thinking now?

John: I'm still thinking about it.

Michael: See, I think Mal is nearest to it: in effect it should be entertainment for the world, and therefore it should be the most entertaining show featuring the four of you… It should be great, great showbiz because that's what's going to make people happy… A smile on the lips of a small boy in France, or a tear in the eye of a big girl in America, is what we all want. 'Cos entertainment is what we're all selling.

Laughing.

Michael: Right?

George: [sings] 'That's entertainment!'

Paul: There's certain basic things we've just got to do if we're going to do it… As far as I can see it, there's only two ways – and that's what I was shouting about in the last meeting we had. There's only two things, you know. We're going to do it, or we're not going to do it. And I want a decision. Because I'm not interested enough to [witheringly] spend

my fucking days farting round here while everyone makes up their minds whether they want to do it or not, you know. I'll do it. If everyone else will, and everyone wants to do it, then all right. But, [laughs] you know, [laughs] it's just a bit soft. It's like at school, you know. You've got to be here! And I *haven't*! You know, I've left school. We've all left school and you don't have to go.

A few moments later…

Paul: … 'The [White] Album' was like this, you see.

Michael: What, agony?

Paul: Well, just the whole idea of 'Do you want to do it? Do we want to do it?' And that's the joke, you see. After it all came about apparently Neil [Aspinall] was saying we'd all phoned him individually, saying things like, 'Can you get 'em together?' You know, 'Can you get it together? I want to know – what are we doing, you know?' Instead of asking each other, we'd all gone to Neil and asked him, you know: 'What are the lads doing?' But, you know, we should just have it out.

George: But we keep coming up against that one and I keep saying, 'Yeah well, I'd like to do this, this, and that. And I'd like to do this. And I'd like to do that. And I'd like to do that.' And we end up doing something again that nobody really wants to do. [laughs]

Paul: Well then, you know, if this one turns into that, it should definitely be the last for all of us because there just isn't any point.

John: I mean, I'm not…

George: Yeah, that's it.

Michael: I think that'd be sad. I mean, as an audience that'd be sad.

Paul: Course it is! It's stupid…

The people who are being stupid are the four of us. There's nobody else…

George: Just being creative instead of being, you know, like, in the doldrums, which it always is, you know.

Michael: I wrote in my book… 'cos I kind of keep a diary of what's going on, so I can cut it, and 'doldrums' is a word I used. 'Cos the doldrums have been coming like to a ship on a…

George: Oh, The Beatles have been in the doldrums for at least a year.

Michael: You see, that is terribly sad.

Paul: But, I mean, we haven't played together, you see, that's the fucking thing. But when we do come together to play together, we all just sort of talk about the fucking past! We're like old age pensioners! [Speaks as if he has no teeth] 'Remember the days when we used to rock!' You know, but we're here now, we can do it… All I want to see is enthusiasm!

Mal: I'd just like to say that you are needed, you know. The Beatles are needed, like, to so many people.

A little later.

Paul: See, it doesn't matter what's going wrong. It really doesn't matter what's going wrong as long as the four of us notice it.

George: I've [laughs] noticed it all right!

Paul: No, but, and… you know… instead of just noticing it, determined to put it right… That's what I'm onto.

George: I think we should have a divorce.

Paul: Well, I said that at the last meeting. But it's getting near it, you know.

John: Who'd have the children?

Paul: Dick James.

John: Oh yeah.

Paul: 'Cos, you know, that's what I was telling you on the phone, that I'll do it, you know, just because it is so silly for us now, at this point in our lives, to crack up. It's just so silly. Because there's no point. We're not going to get anywhere that we want to get by doing that. The only possible direction is the other way from that, you know. But the thing is, we're just all sort of theoretically agreeing with it, but not doing it, you know.

The band rehearse 'I've Got A Feeling' extensively. They move on to 'The Long And Winding Road', 'Oh! Darling' and 'Maxwell's Silver Hammer', before the day's work finishes.

WEDNESDAY
8 JANUARY
1969

George, Ringo and Michael are talking.
George: 'I Me Mine', it's called.
Ringo: Right.
George: [unfolding notes] Shall I sing it to you? I don't care if you don't want it on your show. I don't give a fuck! It can go in my musical. [strums] It's a heavy waltz. [laughs]
Ringo: Mmm. [claps in waltz time]
George: [sings] 'All through the day/ I me mine, I me mine, I me mine/ All through the night/ I me mine, I me mine, I me mine/ Now they're frightened of leaving it/ Everyone's weaving it/ Coming on strong all the time/ All through the day/ I me mine…'
They talk about last night's television.
Ringo: Did you watch the BBC2 thing?
George: Yeah. There was that science fiction thing [an episode of a sci-fi series titled *Out of the Unknown*]. But then suddenly it turned into all that crap about medals and things. Did you see that?
Michael: Yeah, we saw that. I saw that. Yeah. Yeah.

Out of the Unknown *was followed by* Europa: The Titled and the Unentitled, *a programme made by French TV about the British honours system, and the forthcoming investiture of the Prince of Wales.*
George: So, that was on and that's what gave me the idea, 'cos suddenly it was the bit where they were all coming into the ball, I think it was Austria, and they all had their medals on, and there was some music playing… music like a three/four thing. And some things like that happen – where you just hear something and it registers in your head as something else. And so I just had that in my head, just the waltz thing, and

it was fitting [sings] 'I Me Mine'. There were no words to it. I just…
Michael: It's very catchy. It's good.

Enter Paul, John and Yoko, and George Martin. The band work on 'Two Of Us', 'Don't Let Me Down', 'I've Got A Feeling', and 'One After 909'.
Paul: Anyone else…?
George: Where's the paper?
John: 'Queen says "No" to pot-smoking FBI members'.
Laughing.
George: You've got 'Across The Universe', 'Maxwell's Hammer', 'All Things Must Pass', and then… 'She Said She Said'.
The band fall into a spontaneous – and brief – version of 'She Said She Said'. They go to work on 'She Came In Through The Bathroom Window', 'All Things Must Pass', 'Mean Mr Mustard' (with its original line about 'his sister Shirley'), and 'Don't Let Me Down'.
Paul: Okay?
John: Fine, thanks.
Paul: Just drop it.
John: Go on, Harrison.
George: Okay.
John: Lift us out of this mire.

The band return to 'All Things Must Pass'. They go on to 'She Came In Through The Bathroom Window', before they play 'Maxwell's Silver Hammer', and 'I Me Mine'. They put down their instruments. Standing up, John and Paul begin talking.

Paul: [theatrically] We're gonna be faced with a crisis, you know.

John: [equally theatrically] When I'm up against the wall, Paul, you'll find I'm at my best.

Paul: [shouting] Yeah, I know, John, I know, but I just wish you'd come up with the goods!

John: Well, look, I think I've got Sunday off!

Paul: Yeah, well, I hope you can deliver.

John: I'm hoping for a little rock'n'roller.

Paul: Yeah, I was hoping for the same thing myself, you know.

George: Oh, is this on echo?

Paul: Yep. It's so exciting, you know, these new developments in egotronics.

John: [singing] 'Don't bother me, don't bother me…'

George: I remember [writing] that on my sick bed in Bournemouth! You know, I was in bed at Bournemouth when we were on a summer season… [laughs]

Ringo: You were always ill when we were working.

George: The doctor gave me some tonic which must have had amphetamine or something in it. Remember? And you all drank it to get high. And that's when I wrote that one… I met some fella, well, a month ago, at the traffic lights in a car saying, 'Hi man, remember me? Royston Ellis, Gambier Terrace. Gave you your first drugs…'

Paul leads the band through 'Oh! Darling' and 'Let It Be', played much faster than the final version.

George: That song…

Paul: What?

George: That song… Give it to Aretha Franklin…

Paul: Do it *and* give it to her… As soon as we've got it, then we should get the tapes and do a rough demo when it's the first rehearsal. [inaudible]… trying to get her to sing it. It'd be great for Aretha Franklin, that number.

After a while, talk turns to the show.

Michael: We seem to be rejecting the richer ideas, and I think therefore we're back to the simplest idea.

Yoko: [giggles] 'The richer ideas…'

Paul: What do we have as an audience, then?

Michael: Human beings.

John: [posh accent] A group of pastry cooks from Walton-on-Thames!

Michael: And what's going to be our mind-blasting topper at the end? Which I think ought to be a weepy myself.

Ringo: No. Go out with a bang!

Michael: Go out with a bang? Or a cry?

Paul: Well, you know, we intend to write a couple of rockers.

Michael: I think you should open exciting, and end with the audience in tears.

Some time later, Michael and Ringo fall into conversation, as Paul and George work on 'The Long And Winding Road'…

Michael: The thing is, everything you do has got to be good 'cos all your albums are good. I mean there's not a duff album there… And I'm not saying, like, you are the [inaudible] world, or anything like that. But it's got to be the best, because the hearts of millions are with you, you know what I mean? It's got to be the best.

Ringo: It's hard though, 'cos every time we do anything it's got to be really awesome. Maybe we just do something straight… We're playing now anyway like four years ago. We're getting… Suddenly everyone wants to be a rock'n'roller, you know.

Michael: But the audience isn't the same and life isn't the same. I just do find that this place… it could be rock'n'roll, I think, and also it could be this kind of…

Ringo: But I don't think it could be rock'n'roll in Tahiti, or wherever you want to put us. What's it called?

Michael: I don't care: it's either Tunisia or Tripoli.

Ringo: Tunisia?

Michael: Or Tripoli.

Ringo: What about Gibraltar?

As George plays The Band's 'To Kingdom Come', enter Denis O'Dell. A conversation begins around a pile of production notes and set designs. Everyone is standing up.

Denis: I really think we ought to go and shoot a day sequence, a night sequence, a torchlight sequence out there… We'll see the desert, for four days. Make it comfortable for everybody; go over and set it up upfront.

Paul: See, I'll tell you what, though, my main objections to that are travelling, setting up…

Denis: We'll make that comfortable.

Paul: Okay, yeah, so setting up and everything, I'm sure we can do that. Then there's that thing, you know, which may not seem much but it's, like, we're doing a live show and we're doing it in Arabia. [laughs] And whoever has been waiting to see the lads, you know, rocking again… So, I'll tell you what, then: I'll come in with it as long as you can get a couple of boats, like the QE2.

Denis: Yeah, and go over there.

Paul: Give away the tickets here, as you would have done, but the ticket includes a boat journey as well… film on the boat!

Glyn: Fantastic!

Michael: Yeah, we'll do that anyway.

Glyn: What a gas to all the kids, though. A little ride on a boat, and all that.

Paul: Yeah. And for us too!

Laughing.

Glyn: Yeah.

Laughing.

Michael: One of Russia's points was that he wanted an English audience.

George: Oh well, you don't want the Cavern.

Michael: I dig that.

Ringo: Oh, the Cavern's okay… Why don't we just do the show right here? [laughs]

George: [to Michael] Haven't had a holiday this year, eh?

John and Yoko join the conversation.

Michael: [to John] Come on, we're going to Africa!

Denis: We're off! On a boat!

Paul: No, we're not… not necessarily.

Michael: No, we're not.

Ringo: Not quite!

John: [shouting] Yeah! Let's go! Let's go!

Laughing.

Paul: See, if we took a boat… I mean, we…

Denis: I mean, you know, compared with this, it'll be knockout!

We can do this any day. We can do this next Thursday in one day, or two days.

Michael: But we've got to get the right audience for Russia.

Ringo: Yeah. [laughs]

John: Oh, Russia? That'd be great!

Michael: No, no, no, that's Ringo's code name. He's Russia.

George: He said, 'Rush hour.'

John: Oh, rush hour.

Michael: No, Russia… If we get the right audience over there, which we can get over there…

George: Over where?

Michael: Anywhere, if we did it abroad.

George: I don't, I can't… what is the point of doing it abroad?

Michael: I think the point of doing it abroad is that…

George: Apart from getting a quick holiday? I'd much rather do it, and *then* go away.

Paul: [gruff Cockney accent] Now look, if we're going away and we hire a boat to take the audience with you…

Denis: That would be knockout!

Paul: … we'll do a bloody show on the boat…

Michael: On the boat.

Paul: And then we do a show when we get there… in the moonlight!

Michael: Well, hold on. Wait. Here comes France coming in here now.

George: France? I can't go to France!

Michael: No, no, no. That's your code name.

Laughing.

Paul: He smoked some garlic once!

Laughing.

Michael: You see, I don't think anything is going to beat a perfect acoustic place by the water, out of doors, a perfect theatre with perfect…

John: It's just the idea of…

Michael: Acoustics, Glyn! Glyn, hit the acoustics.

John: Just singing a number at sunset…

Glyn: The acoustic situation will be superb!

John: … and at dawn and all that… Just gentle and all the moon, and all that. Just for the songs, you know…

Ringo: For a rock'n'roll group?

John: Yeah.

Michael: I'm sure we can do the rock'n'roll there if we get the right audience. 'Cos if they swing we've got the right audience for rock'n'roll.

Ringo: We'll have to take them with us, then.

John: Well, we'll take a few with us, you know.

Ringo: A boatload!

Michael: A boatload! We all come on a boat.

George: You need a bloody big boat for the gear.

Denis: Yeah.

George: How long is it going to take, then? Then the show's going to take like…

Denis: Well, it'll take three days' trip on the boat getting there.

George: Where to?

Denis: To Sabratha [laughs]… Tripoli! Fantastic sand!

Paul: [comically] Fantastic!

Denis: It'll be cool!

Paul: Yes. And also it's that thing where… last year when we were doing

the album, we suddenly said, 'We don't need to do it here in EMI any longer.'

John: Every time we've done an album we've said, 'Why are we stuck in EMI? [excitedly] We could be doing it in LA, we could be in France.' And every time we do it, and here we are again building another bloody castle round us. And this time we do it there, you know.

Paul: [Scouse accent] Well said, John. Well said!

John: [passionately] And not only would we be doing it, physically making the album there, but it takes all that weight of where, where's the gimmick? What is it? 'Cos, you know… God's the gimmick.

Michael: You're just there and… I mean, it's got a 'copter shot.

John: And the only problem we've got now is an audience, you know.

Paul: I mean, it does make it like an adventure, doesn't it?

John: I'd be thrilled to do it, you know, just for the timing it so as the sun came up just [clicks fingers] just on the middle eight, you know, and all that.

Michael: Which Denis says it does.

John: Yeah, you can do that.

Michael: The sun sinks and the moon comes up over the hill.

John: You know, I can just see us in this…

Michael: It's on the African coast.

John: … this place and just the moon coming up and the smoke blowing…

Ringo: Yeah, well, I just really do feel that we should do it here.

Denis: You would love it. It's a fantastic place.

Ringo: I've stopped being Russia now. And I'm not saying I'm not going.

John: I know what you mean, man. But just give me one reason to stay here.

Ringo: For the people!

Michael: Bring them with us!

John: Okay. The people? That's the only…

Paul: See, that's it. Look, we were going to give tickets away at this door here, and say the first thousand people who come from Britain…

Ringo: Yeah.

Paul: … So we give 'em out those tickets, but they include a boat ride as well.

Denis: Cor!

John: Yeah.

Michael: And we take 'em with us. And that's the show.

George: And you're going to go there on the boat as well?

John: Well, that's developing it into a super-duper…

Paul: I mean, if we're on a boat and those boats have, like, ballrooms…

John: It'd be great, yeah. We do the dress rehearsal on the boat…

Paul: … we'd have a rehearsal.

Denis: Put your name down for this cruise!

Michael: While we're all here and… and we ain't going away, if we can get the audience… if we can get the audience…

Denis: And the boat!

Michael: And the boat, who votes to go? There's one hand.

John: Ja!

Denis: It's gonna be great! You'll love the place!

Ringo: I've moved to Yugoslavia!

Laughing.

Denis: You will love this…

Michael: Just say yes! Just say yes!

Ringo: You know… If you're really going to all that…

George: I may love the place but I'd rather do the show then go and love the place. I just want to get it over with.

John: It'll just take all that weight of what to do with the show, that's the end of it, you know.

Ringo: But I still don't think, you know, that's a hundred percent sure that wherever we go that'll make the show.

Paul: It's got to be filmed, you know, like *[Magical] Mystery Tour*, you know.

George: We're making a film, then.

Paul: I like the two things. The show, you know…

John: No, no, but that's…

George: And then on top of that we're stuck with a bloody big boatload of people for two weeks.

Ringo: Who think they know us!

George: You know, I mean… at least you can go home from here, you can get away from it all.

Denis: When you get there on your own, you'll say, 'I wish I could have played here!'

George: I mean, it's just impractical. It's just impractical to try and lug all them people there and try and get all that equipment.

Paul: But then if it was *their* problem…

Denis: If you say, 'That's what I want,' then that has to happen.

George: Of course it's our problem.

Michael: I think the sense of adventure, Christopher Columbus, will make it. And I don't think there is a gimmick in it.

Paul: I think you're D-A-F-T!

Ringo: No, I think you Americans don't know your roots!

Laughing.

Michael: So how are we stacking? If there's no problem with the equipment, and with the right audience, which will be basically English-speaking [people]

brought from here, I think…

John: Broadminded Englishmen wanted!

A few moments later.

John: See, it's like having the most fantastic set on Earth, but we haven't made a set, you know. That's the bit. It's simplicity itself, but we just happen…

Ringo: How many are going to be looking at the set besides us and him? *Laughing.*

Michael: If you'll say yes and if we get it together, then will you go?

George: If we say yes… [laughs]

Paul: We say yes.

Laughing

John: Well, if we mull it over tonight… Let's have a sort of, er…

Glyn: A mull.

Paul: A mull.

John: Leave it in the air and that, just think about it.

Michael: But I feel, as the trade says, the vibes are very good at the moment about it.

John: Yeah, but I mean we can all say

yes now and somebody can decide no tomorrow.

Denis: Yeah. Tomorrow there's something else…

John: It's not going to make any odds. Let's just think about it.

Denis: I think John's right. I think you should think about it… You've talked about it. You know what you've been doing for three days. What are you going to do for the next six or eight days? So we think about it. Yeah, Ring?

Ringo: I'll be watching telly, actually.

George: I think just the idea of the boat is completely insane!

Denis: It's nice, though, isn't it? It's a nice sort of insanity, though, George.

George: It's very expensive and insane, and we'd have a boatful of…

Denis: I think that should be the least of our worries, money. I really do.

Yoko: Yeah, but going on a boat…

Ringo: I mean it's… how much is this [i.e. Twickenham Film Studios] for a week? Forty thousand and something?

George: It'd have to be a bloody big boat. It'd have to be bigger than the [Mersey ferry] *Royal Iris*.
Laughing.

Ringo: I imagined something like [famous ocean liner] the *Reina del Mar* or something.

John: Aristotle [Onassis]'s yacht, you know. Let Aristotle…

Ringo: That's too small. I want a liner. If we're going on a boat…

John: Aren't they big, those?

George: No. No. You can always just compare boats.

Ringo: No. I want a liner. If we're going on a boat…

George: And who's going to cough up for that, though?

John: P&O will do a deal with [inaudible]…

Paul: Probably isn't as expensive…

John: We should be able to get the boat for the publicity they get from it. If we do a show on a P&O liner…

Denis: You see!

George: They won't even give us a

free Fender amp! [laughs] We've got to buy them!

Ringo: You know, how are you going to get a ship in a couple of days?

Denis: In fucking three hours on the phone we'll know the answer.
Later…

Denis: Are you going to go for dinner?

Paul: I am.

George: [sings] 'Cut out the bullshit! Cut out the bullshit! Cut out the bullshit!'

Paul: Cheerio all!

George: Good night!

Michael: Good night, Russia.

Ringo: That's a wrap!

Denis: I'll see you in Sabratha!

John: Let's pretend I wasn't here again!

**THURSDAY
9 JANUARY
1969**

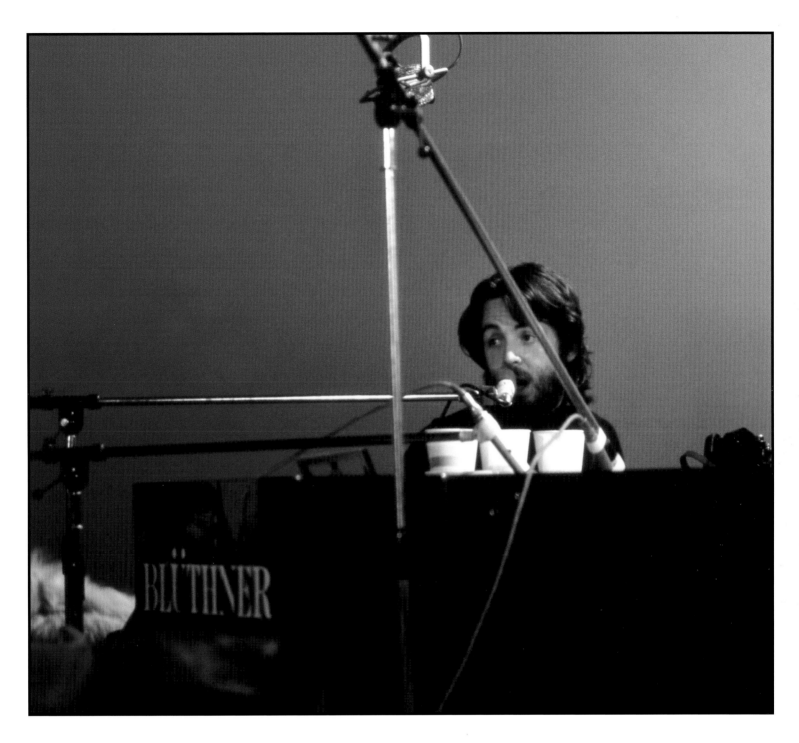

Enter Paul and Linda.
Paul: [to Linda] Do you know Michael Lindsay-Hogg?
Linda: Nope.
Paul: Tony is a cameraman.
Tony: Hi.
Paul: Linda's a cameraman.
Tony: Nice. Nice to meet a cameraman.
Linda: [to Paul] So if you do it [i.e. the show], it would be in here?
Paul: I don't know. There's many a story…
Linda: I mean, you could do it here.
Paul: But if we don't, it's on a boat to Tripoli.

Paul goes to the piano, and begins playing an early version of 'Another Day', the song he will release as his first solo single.
Paul: [sings] 'In the morning [inaudible] when she takes a break/ Makes a cup of coffee and she finds it hard to stay awake/ It's just another day… At the office where the papers grow she takes a break/ De-de-de-der and she finds it hard to stay awake/ It's just another day…'
Sound of castanets.
Paul: [to Mal] You just do a rattle.
Mal: [laughs] Yeah.

More castanets.
Mal: Have you heard, er, Bonzo Dog – 'Urban Spaceman'?
Paul: Heard it? I produced it!
Mal: Did you?
Paul: Yeah.
Mal: Do you have any more words to write out? More songs?
Paul: Yeah. [sings] 'When I find myself in times of trouble, Mother Mary comes to me/ Speaking words of wisdom/ Let it be/ And in my hour of darkness she is standing right in front of me/ Speaking words of wisdom/ Let it be…'

He segues into 'The Long And Winding Road', still missing its second verse and finished lyrics for its middle eight.
Paul: [sings] 'I have had some pleasure from the many ways… the many ways I've tried/ But still they… Still they lead me back to the long winding road/ You left me waiting here a long, long time ago…'
Ringo: Use 'standing'.
Paul: You like 'standing' better?
Ringo: Well, yeah.
Mal: Yeah, put 'waiting' there, and 'standing' there.
Paul: I was thinking of that, yeah.
Mal: What did you think of where to do the show? What did you think about last night? I think it's down to, if you're going to do it in this country you might as well do it here.
Ringo: I went off the boat, actually, the idea.
Mal: Yeah.
Ringo: Just because I'm, like…
Are we going to just hire a ship and [inaudible]…
Mal: You're not going to get people on the thing to…
Ringo: We know what it's like on holiday. You know, I go a bit crazy.
Mal: So if we do it in this country, I think it should be here.
Ringo: In this actual building?
Mal: Yeah.

Paul: The airport and the Houses of Parliament aren't the right ones, you know. But if we hit the right one, then…
Mal: Do it in the cathedral.
Ringo: Shaftesbury Cathedral.
Mal: But, you see… people who do things in places where they're not normally doing 'em – that's a bit contrived as well, you know.
Paul: Yes, right.

Still at the piano, Paul begins playing 'Her Majesty', then 'Golden Slumbers'.
Paul: Should be ready for a *Songs For Swinging Lovers!* album soon.
Laughing.
Paul is referring to Frank Sinatra's classic 1956 album.
Paul: It's an old English folk song – the words.
'Golden Slumbers' segues into 'Carry That Weight'.
Paul: Listen to this 'Carry That Weight' bit. If you can think of a little bit… like a story. A bit like 'Act Naturally' where you sort of… [slurps tea]… The tag line keeps coming up, you know, and then so-and-so and so-and-so, but all they said was 'All you gotta do is act naturally'. So it'd belike, you know…[singing] 'The trouble in the world made me get in trouble again… I hang my head at the end of the day and I knew that/ But every time I go to the [inaudible]… He said,

"Boy you're gonna carry that weight/ Carry that weight a long time"…'
Like their troubles.
Ringo: Yeah.
Paul: You know, all my troubles. But… it was like a comedy when I heard it. You know, it was like… [sings] 'Boy, you're gonna carry that weight/ Carry that weight a long time/ Boy, you're gonna carry that weight/ Carry that weight a long time/ When I get drunk tonight [inaudible] downstairs/ She said [inaudible] morning "Do not drink in here"/ I said, "Now baby, you think you know it all"/ Every time I try to do…' See, that could, like, be a verse about, like, got drunk, got in trouble with the wife, got drunk, so-and-so and so-and-so, and then woke up the next morning with a weight upon my head, and I found out it, it *was* my head!
Mal: [returning to the lyric of 'The Long And Winding Road'] Do you want to finish this? Have you got any idea for the second verse?
Paul: Er, no. Erm…

Paul plays piano and sings 'The Long And Winding Road'.
Paul: [sings] 'Many times I've been alone and many times I've cried/ La-la-la-la-la-la the many ways I've tried…' That's all right. 'The many ways I've tried', I like.

Paul plays 'Oh! Darling'. Enter George.
Ringo: Morning, George.
George: Hiya, lads. I was just so hungry today, I had to be late just to eat my breakfast… if you wanted an excuse. [laughs]

Having accompanied Paul's piano playing on the drums, George picks up his guitar and plays 'For You Blue'. Paul soon joins in on piano, followed by Ringo. John and Yoko arrive. John eats a slice of toast.
John: [to Ringo] There's a house by you which I fancy.
Ringo: Lloyd George's?
John: Yeah. So I'll pop in for a cup of tea if I come round, Saturday or Sunday… It sounds all right, it sounds like only about the same size as [John's house in] Weybridge. It was built for him in about forty acres as well.
Linda: Forty acres!
John: And about three lakes.

Linda: Oooooh.
John: You know, like, all joined together. So sounds good. £45,000.
Ringo: Sounds amazing!
John: Yeah.
Linda: Forty acres!
John: You press a button and iron gates shut on all the windows, you know, in case they get in.
A few moments later.
John: [to George] Shall we learn your song, then?
George: Which one?
John: That 'I love you sweet and honey baby'…
George: As well? I mean, I've used three… [laughs]
John: You can do as many as you like.
Paul: Let's run through the ones we know, then.
John: [raspy voice] Songs we know… Yes. Okay, well, we can do 'Across The Universe'. I'm going to have to learn the words.

Paul: Shall we do 'Two Of Us'?
The band play 'Two Of Us', in its initial fast form, with Paul standing up.
Paul: It's still, still… it's still pathetic… Well, after that I collapse and sit down for 'Don't Let Me Down'!
Mal: Paul? Do you want to listen to a playback before you do it?
Paul: Er…
John: [witchy voice] Not just yet, Mal. I'd like another cuppa of our tea, like. Not that piss-pot stuff they serve here, you know.
George: Do you have access to real tea?
John: I've got nice tea with us…

They play 'Don't Let Me Down',
'I've Got A Feeling', 'Suzy Parker'
and 'One After 909'.

George: While we're on the ramblers, we might as well do the one about the window.

Paul: 'She Came In Through The Bathroom Window'.

John: I'd just like to talk for a few moments while John goes over on piano.

Paul: [imitating Elvis] All I'm saying is it's a great occasion for us and I must say that…

Ringo: [American accent] It's the first chance we've had to play to you dummies for a long time.

Laughing.

Paul: Just great!

Later, Paul is working on the lyrics for 'Get Back'…

Paul: [sings] 'Ho-ni-no-ni-no-ni thought she was a woman, but she was another man/ All the folks around said she got it coming, but she get it while she can/ Oh get back, get back, get back to where you once belonged/ Get back, get back, get back to where you once belonged…' We might get it into something with words, but we'll just keep doing it just like that, though.

George: Yeah, like this, yeah.

Paul: 'Cos it started off like that and it's gone [plays]… It's something about 'I left my home in Arizona, de, de, de, de, de…'

George: Oh so… 'Get back, get back…'

Paul: … 'Get back to where you once belonged'

George laughs.

Paul: Think of some words if you can.

George: Erm…

Paul: I don't know what it's about. It's about going away, and then the chorus is 'Get back!'

George: Er…

Paul: So I just… Actually, it's not about anything.

Laughing.

Paul: You know…

John: A hot woman!

George: Yeah, we'll just have those words; just words that, like that [song by The Band] 'Caledonia Mission'. They're just nothing about anything. It's just, like, rubbish. As long as it's nice to say.

Some time later…
John: Well, good afternoon, I'd like to welcome you to the rehearsal rooms of The Beatles' entourage and their fifty press officers, where they're just breaking into a number called 'Across The Unicorn'.

The band rehearse 'Across The Universe', before breaking into a rendition of 'The House Of The Rising Sun'. Paul then begins improvising satirical lyrics about Enoch Powell, the Conservative politician whose infamous, racist 'Rivers of Blood' speech – made in April 1968 – led to his sacking from the shadow cabinet by Conservative leader Ted Heath.

Paul: [sings, in the manner of a pub performer] 'Tonight Enoch Powell said, "Get out immigrants!/ Immigrants had better go home!" Ah-ha-ha-ha… Tonight Harold Wilson said to the immigrants, "You'd better get back to your Commonwealth homes!"/ Yeah, yeah, yeah!/ He said, "You'd better get back home!"… Now Enoch Powell – well, he said to the folks, he said he knew the colour of your skin/ He said, he don't care what it's all about… So Ted Heath said to Enoch Powell – he said, "You'd better get on, or else… Enoch, you'd better go home!"'

Paul carries on singing and playing, accompanied by John. Yoko dances in her seat.
Paul: [singing] 'Commonwealth!'
John: [in high-pitched, pantomime-dame voice] 'Yes?'
Paul: [laughing] 'Commonwealth!'
John: 'Yes?'
Paul: 'Commonwealth!'
John: 'Yes?'

Paul: 'Commonwealth!'
John: 'Yes?'
Paul: 'If you don't want trouble then you better go back to home…'
He begins improvising a verse.
Paul: [in Cockney accent] 'So I went to Pakistani [*sic*]/ I went to India/ I've been to Old Calcutta and I've had enough of that!/ I'm comin' back to England town.'
John: 'Yes, welcome!'
Paul: 'And dirty Enoch Powell! And he's had enough of coloured men! Oh, Commonwealth!'
John: 'Yes?'
Paul: 'Commonwealth!'
John: 'Yes?'
Paul: 'Yeah, Commonwealth!'
John: 'Yes?'
Paul: 'Oh hear me talkin' Commonwealth!/ Yeah, the Commonwealth, but it's much too wealthy for me!…'
John: [speaking] Much too *common* for me.
Paul: [singing] 'I ambled down Australia and New Zealand too/ I only took to Pakistan and India too/ I came back to West Indies and I had a cricket match/ I went out to South Africa and turned into the patch/ Oh Commonwealth, you're much too common for me!/ Everybody sing! Well, Commonwealth! Yeah, Commonwealth!'
John: 'Yeah?'
Paul: 'Enoch Powell, Commonwealth!'
John: 'Yeah!'
Paul: 'Immigrants, Commonwealth!'
John: 'Yeah!'
Paul: 'Well I would join the Common Market but it's much too common for me…'
The tempo drops.
Paul: [sings] 'Oh Enoch Powell… Oh Enoch Powell… *Powerless.*'

FRIDAY
10 JANUARY
1969

Enter Paul, Ringo, Glyn Johns, Michael Lindsay-Hogg and Dick James, Managing Director of Northern Songs. They sit down and talk.

Dick: Good morning, Ringo.
Ringo: Morning, Dick.
Dick: How are you?
Ringo: Not so bad.
Paul: Did you see Peter Cook [on TV] last night?
Ringo: Yes, he was great.
Dick: Great, wasn't it?
Paul: 'What do you think of Zsa Zsa Gabor?' Eamonn [Andrews, chat show host] asked him. He said, 'Oh, you want the truth? I think she's vain, untalented, a non-event.' [laughs]… with his right eyebrow shaking like mad [laughs]. Terrible. She said, 'I tink you are ze rudest man I have ever seen.'
Dick: Oh, she was there, was she?
Paul: Oh sure, she was there.
Ringo: Peter said, 'That's because I tell the truth, darling.'
Paul: What did you think…?
Michael: That's called sock it to 'em, isn't it?
Paul: She's quite entertaining. One thing I don't like her for is, she was with her daughter… her daughter was always around EMI when we were making the last album. And we saw Zsa Zsa with her daughter there, and she

makes a sort of ass out of her daughter. She's so honest… She sort of said, you know, 'Don't wear that sweater, darling,' when we were all there, you know. 'Don't wear that sweater, it makes you look fat.' And she is a bit sort of fat.
Michael: I hate parents that put their kid down…
Dick: It's a wonder the daughter didn't use a four-letter word to the mother.
A little later…
Dick: How about the 'Ob-La-Di, Ob La-Da' covers and things? All right?
Paul: Yes, doing well, yeah.
Dick: Erm… I'll pop some records, you know, over to the flat – just in case you'd like to hear it – of Vera Lynn's 'Good Night' as a waltz. Stephen [James] produced it. It's done as a three/four. Sounds beautiful.
Paul: Ringo'd like to hear that.
Dick: You'd like to hear that, would you, Ringo?
Paul: Yeah.
Ringo: Yes, love to.
Michael: [yawns] Have there been many covers of 'Good Night'?
Paul: No. I think this is the first cover.
Michael: I thought there would have been more on there.
Enter George.
George: Hi!
Ringo: Hiya, George.
Paul: Hiya, George.

George: Hiya, people.
Dick: Hi, George.
George: Hello, Dick.
Dick: [enthusiastically] How are you? Happy New, er… Happy Soixante-Neuf.
George: And the same to you, Dick… Thanks for the present.
Dick: You're very welcome.
George: Very nice glasses, those.
Dick: Yes. Useful. Something to drink out of… or the wife can throw.
Paul: I didn't get any glasses.
Dick: You did, you know.
Paul: Did I?
George: They're probably still in the office.
Dick: If you didn't, someone stuck to 'em. You know I don't discern among [*sic*] my friends.

Paul plays 'The Long And Winding Road' at the piano. Enter John and Yoko.

Dick: Are you likely to be home tomorrow evening watching television?

John: Why? What's on?

Dick: Er, the Rolf Harris Show. Vera Lynn's on, singing 'Good Night'. The record's out today.

John: I thought she'd done 'The Fool On The Hill'.

Dick: B-side.

John: Oh, amazing. That's very good.

Dick: Yeah. We've put 'em back-to-back. So tomorrow night…

John: That'd be nice, if she gets a hit with that.

George: [to Dick] You haven't got an [US soul singer] Arthur Conley version of 'Ob-La-Di', have you?

Dick: Well, I'll check… A what?

George: 'Ob-La-Di' by Arthur Conley. That'll be the big American one.

Dick: Oh, yes, it's, er… I think it's about number 61, or 51…

George: Is it?

Dick: It came in at 100…

George: It came in at 79, I thought.

Dick: [to Ringo] Still driving the Merc? You've got the black one, haven't you?

Ringo: No. Silver.

The band rehearse 'I've Got A Feeling'. Paul asks John about his recent appearances with Yoko in a giant bag.

Paul: Can you see each other in the bag?

John: Yes [laughs].

Paul: When you're in the bag?

John: Yes. We're together in a bag.

Paul: I know. But can you see each other inside when you're in the bag?

John: Yes, yes. It's just like being under the sheets, you know.

Paul: Yes, I suppose… It's great.

John: She generally used to use black bags.

Yoko: It was scary, though…

The band work on 'Get Back', which is still at an early stage, without clear lyrics, and yet to acquire its shuffling rhythm.

George: Do you want me to do that… accentuate that beat of the drum?

Paul: Yeah. See, the thing is, though, just for the three of us – that's good enough for the rock'n'roll thing. But then, you know, I think then…

George: You need Eric Clapton playing on top of it.

Paul: No. You don't. You need, like, a…

John: George Harrison.

Paul: You need George Harrison, but just doing simple things until it's your go, you know… Because otherwise you get the guitar conflicting with what you're singing, and all that.

George: Yeah.

Paul: And then I'm trying to sing louder to get over the guitar. But really it should also go…

George: Well, really you only need one guitar.

Paul: Yeah. But if you do the offbeat [hits chord] with Ringo, and you got that more and in the [sings and plays] 'Get back, get back…', then let us do that bit…

A few minutes later…

Paul: [to John] I'll tell you the words, then.

John: Yeah, okay. I'll just write it down.

Paul: Well, the gist of it so far [is], 'Well, get back to where you belonged.'

John: Yeah…

Paul: [sings] 'Sweet Loretta Marsh she thought she was a woman/ But she was another man/ Sweet Loretta Marsh she thought she had it coming but she got it while she can…'

John: 'Sweet Loretta Marsh thought she was a woman but she was another man'?

Paul dictates the lyrics as John writes them down.

Paul: 'But she was another man…' Er… 'All the folks around her say she's got it coming, but she's got it while she can… she gets it while she can…'

John: [sings] 'Say she's got it coming.'

Paul: 'She gets it while she can.' It fits, actually.

John: Yeah.

Paul: It's a drag queen, you know, and 'Get back to where you once belonged…'

John: Yeah.

Paul: It's like, you do have a few problems, you know.

A few moments later…

Paul: [sings] '… left his home in Arizona…'… Joey Blues… Joey [inaudible].

John: Oh, another one. Joey rah-dah dah-dah…

Paul: [sings] 'Jo Jo when he left is…' So what's the…

John: Jo Jo, with a last name.

Paul: What's the name? Jo Jo…?

John: Gumm.

Paul: [sings and plays] 'Jo Jo Lemon… Jo Jo Clark and Jo Jo Williams… Jo Jo…'

John: Jo Jo Dandy.

Paul: [sings] 'Jo Jo Jackson left his home in Arizona…' Jo Jo Jackson?

John: Yeah.

Paul: [sings] 'Jo Jo Jackson left his

home in Arizona, but dah, dah, dah…'

John: 'But he knew it wouldn't last.'

Paul: Well, see, we can get better words.

The band move on to 'Two Of Us', still played with a fast rock arrangement. They repeatedly go over the 'On our way back home' passage at the end of the verses.

Paul: It needs something else.

John: [singing] '… standing solo in the sun.'

Paul: It does need something else, but that's the…

George: That's the best so far.

Paul: Yeah.

John: It needs sort of… leg movement.

Paul: Yeah. [laughs]

John/Paul: [singing] 'On our way back home/ On our way back home/ On our way back home…'

Paul: It's near enough.

John plays loud guitar.

Paul: That's it, you know. I think it needs a bit more of that, this one. In fact, maybe you should both do that. Could you just stop playing for a minute, John…

John: Yes, all right, Paul!

Paul: [stagily]… while I'm trying to talk to you about this arrangement. Thank you. Shall we go for lunch?

John: [posh accent] Is it lunch already?

Guitar.

Paul: It certainly is.

Sound of the guitar riff from Chuck Berry's 'I'm Talking About You'.

George: I think I'll be… I'm leaving…

John: [stops playing] What?

George: … the band now.

John: When?

George: Now.

The tape suddenly resumes.

George: … a replacement. Write in to the *NME* and get a few people.

Mal: I'll ask George [Martin] to see about paying residuals…

George: Er… but he shouldn't be bothered with that, you know. That's why we've got Apple, so that, you know, we attend to it ourselves.

Mal: Yeah.

John: We aim to please.

George: Do you know whose this case is?

Mal: Er… Whose case is this, Kevin?

Tony: Hmm. Are you still turning? Hmm?

Unidentified voice: Cut.

Footsteps and whistling.
Exit George.

APPLE FILMS LTD.
BEATLES- DAY 9.
14·1·69   DAY INT.
238   1.
          CAMERA. A
DIR: CAM:
M. LINDSAY HOGG   T. RICHMOND

TUESDAY
14 JANUARY
1969

Some time later. Acoustic guitars, coughing.

Paul: I don't know what we're coming back here for.

John: [laughs] No. Just pretending nothing's happened.

Paul: Yeah. What? Oh, I never saw him [George]. Did he?

Coughing.

Paul: [sounding surprised] I thought he was just going home to get a plec.

John begins playing a section of The Who's 'A Quick One While He's Away'.

John: [sings] 'Soon be home/ Soon be home/ Soon, soon, soon be home…'

Ringo: We have to play harder as a trio!

John: What?

Ringo: We have to play harder as a trio!

John: Yes!

Watched by Maureen Starkey, John, Paul and Ringo jam with Yoko, who contributes wailing vocals. They move on to ferocious, aggressive, and clearly tongue-in-cheek readings of 'I've Got A Feeling' and 'Don't Let Me Down', followed by an aborted go at Eddie Cochran's 'C'mon Everybody'. In the company of George Martin, talk eventually turns to what to do next.

John: I think if George doesn't come back by Monday or Tuesday we ask Eric Clapton to play. I mean, he would [inaudible]… I mean, if George leaves the group…

Ringo: Why did he leave the Cream?

John: Eric'd be pleased to join us. He left Cream because they're all…

Ringo: All soloists.

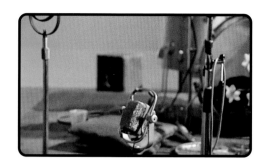

John: … all soloists. But we're not in our group. He'd have full scope to play his guitar. Now the point is, if George leaves, do we want to carry on with The Beatles? I do.

Neil: Anyway, we'll be seeing him Saturday or Sunday, you know.

Michael: But what's the consensus? Do you want to go on with the show and the work?

John: Yes. If he doesn't come back by Tuesday we get Clapton.

After Paul has started playing 'Martha My Dear', Yoko sings along with his piano, repeatedly singing the word 'John' – to which he initially answers 'Yoko!'

Michael: Has anyone ever left as seriously as George before?

John: [quietly] Well, Ringo [has]… We'll see how the weekend goes. There's a meeting.

Michael: I don't know. I was going to say, if George comes back we go away [i.e. abroad, to do the show], and if Clapton comes in we stay here. But I think if… I still think we should go away.

John: We should just go on, though, as if nothing's happened.

Michael: I think we should go away.

More jamming with Yoko, on which Paul plays piano, followed by drums.

Some time later…

Michael: It's looking like rehearsal's over. Would I be right in feeling that?

Ringo: Yep. I feel that.

John: I think your general attitude is right.

Paul: [sings] 'I've got a feeling…'

Michael: I've got a feeling too, that that's it. Well, are we meeting again on Monday?

John: Yeah.

Michael: Just us chickens?

John: I'll have Eric, Jimi and Tommy Marshall…

Paul: [to Maureen] A-7th, D-7th, G-7th. Get 'em off over the weekend, and you're in.

Michael: I guess that's it until the weekend.

Paul: Gotcha.

Michael: Have a nice meeting.

Paul: Okay, Daddy.

Michael: And I hope everything really goes swell.

Paul: Adios.

Michael: I'd like to say I've enjoyed our week together.

Paul: Groovy, Chunky.

Michael: I hope one day we can have another one like it.

Paul: Surely. Surely. Why not.

Michael: So long.

MONDAY 13 JANUARY 1969

Enter Ringo and Tony Richmond.
Tony: What's going to happen?
Is the show still going to happen,
do you think?
Ringo: [looking at a sheet of negatives]
That's why we're here today.
Tony: That's good.
Ringo: To see what…
Tony: To see what can be done?
Ringo: Mmm. [heavy sigh]

*Enter Mal Evans and Glyn. They are
eventually joined by Kevin Harrington
and Michael Lindsay-Hogg.*
Michael: I wonder if we'll see Africa
this time round in our lives.
Laughing.
Ringo: Have you got enough for
a good documentary?
Michael: Well, yes. It depends what
we're allowed to use, if you know what
I mean. It depends how liquid the
situation is. If we tell it like it is, baby…
sock it to 'em… then we've got a very
good documentary. But if…
Ringo: If we're hiding…
Michael: If we're hiding – yeah, that's

the word I was fishing for but not being
brave enough to say. If we're hiding
then we don't have much…We just
have a couple of days when things
didn't work out, that's it. [laughs]…
We just have an apple rind. An apple
rind, as opposed to an apple core.
Ringo: An apple pip.
Laughing.

*Paul and Linda arrive. In between
chatting, everyone listens to a vinyl
copy of Arthur Conley's version
of 'Ob-La-Di, Ob-La-Da'. Enter
Neil Aspinall.*
Ringo: Good morning, Neil.
Neil: Morning. So what's happening?
Ringo: We're just carrying on with the
documentary.
Paul: We're just recording. I just
thought, like, you know, just sing a few
words for the songs that we haven't got
words for and stuff, you know, just to
rehearse them a bit more.
Ringo: For what?
Paul: Dunno. It doesn't matter, though,
you know. If we do an extra week, and

then we decide to chuck it in, just with
the decision that near… and then we
would have really had to split and then
see in a year's time.
Ringo: It's good you've sort of said,
'Come to work'… I'd have been *there*
[i.e. at home], you'd have been down
here, and…
Paul: That's what I thought. I just
thought, What am I going to do
tomorrow?
Ringo: I was going to lie in, actually.
Paul: Yeah.
Linda: Yeah. Sit on the lawn.
Ringo: Do the garden.
Laughing.
Linda: Paint the ceiling.
Ringo: [to Neil] Did you get in touch
with John?
Neil: Mal did, this morning, apparently.
Linda: That's the answering service.
Neil: I couldn't get him.
Michael: Is he joining us?
Ringo: We don't know…
Neil: I haven't spoken to him.
Nobody answers his phone.

Sitting in a circle, they begin talking about the band meeting that happened the previous day at Ringo's house, and John's relationship with Yoko.

Paul: There's, like, always only two answers: one is to fight it and fight her and try and get The Beatles back to four people without Yoko, and sort of ask Yoko to sit down at the board meetings. Or else the other thing is just to realise she's there, you know, and he's not going to sort of split with her just for our sakes. And then it's not even so much of an obstacle, as long as we're not trying to surmount it. You know, while we're still trying to get over it, it's an obstacle. But it isn't really, it's not that bad, you know. They want to stay together, those two, you know. So it's all right, let the young lovers stay together, you know. But it shouldn't be, [Scouse accent] 'We can't operate under these conditions, boy, you know, we're coming out.' It's like we're striking, that's what it is. It's like a strike because work conditions aren't right.

Michael: Mmm.

Paul: But it's not that bad, you know.

Michael: But he knows that, doesn't he?

Paul: John knows that, sure. But he's…

Michael: Does he talk about it at all?

Paul: No. But he's… You see, we've done a lot of Beatles now, we've had a lot of Beatles, you know… so that I think John's thing now… obviously, if it came to a push between Yoko and The Beatles, it's Yoko, you know.

Michael: But funnily enough, the other day when we were talking he said that he really did not want *not* to be a Beatle.

Paul: No, no.

Paul talks to Neil about songwriting.

Paul: It's like we did 'I Will' [from 'The White Album'], and we were trying to get the last verse, and eventually I just ended up doing it, 'cos we couldn't actually do it. But Yoko really tried to stay out of it – just sort of got on with something. But she just really… you know, they're onto that thing; they just want to be near each other. So I just think it's just silly of me or anyone to try and say to 'em, 'No, you can't,' you know.

Neil: Oh yeah.

Paul: 'Cos okay, you know, they're going overboard about it, but John always does, you know, and Yoko probably always does. So that's their scene. You can't go saying, 'Don't go overboard about this thing, be sensible about it and don't bring her to meetings.' It's his decision, that. It's none of our business starting to interfere in that. Even when it comes into our business, you still can't really say much, except, 'Look, I don't like it, John.' You know, then he can say, 'Well, screw you,' or, 'I like it,' or, 'Well, I won't do it,' or something, or blah de blah. But the only way, you know, is to tell John about it.

Michael: Have you done that already?

Paul: Well, I told him I didn't like writing songs… with him and Yoko.

Michael: Were you writing together much more before she came around?

Paul: Oh, yeah. For sure.

Michael: Or had you cooled it a bit then, before her?

Ringo: Before, you'd cooled it a bit.

Paul: Yeah. Cooled it, cooled it, sure. We'd cooled it because of not playing together. Ever since we didn't play together…

Michael: On stage, you mean?

Paul: Yes, because I mean we lived together when we played together – we were in the same hotel, up at the same time every morning doing this all day. And… it doesn't matter what you do… just as long as you're this close all day, something grows, you know. And then when you're not this close then just physically something goes… Actually, musically, you know, we can play better than we've ever been able to play. I really think that.

Michael: Mmm.

Paul: I thought we should just work a lot – you know, really, really get back into that sort of… into the slog, you know… really just, I mean a job, you know, almost nine to five.

Some time later…

Paul: It's going to be such an incredible sort of comical thing like, in fifty years' time, you know: 'They broke up 'cos Yoko sat on an amp,' you know [laughs]… or just something like that. What? 'Well, you see, John kept bringing this girl along.' What? It's not as though there's any sort of earth-splitting rows or anything.

Ringo: Hatchet in the head.

Paul: There's nothing wrong really, just sort of…

Michael: But, like Linda was saying, it really is terribly dispiriting if it doesn't get better, it really is.

Linda: Just music-wise.

Paul: I was talking to Neil last night about an idea that I thought of, for a TV show, but he sort of really finished the idea off, which was…

Michael: Gross, was it? [laughs] What was it?

Paul: No, [he] made it sensational, which was that while we were rehearsing the show ourselves, we should have alongside us someone sort of near, so that we're getting the same kind of buzz, but really completely independent. We should get, say, the editor of the *Daily Mirror* – you'd have to get someone as good as him, a real hard news nut – rehearsing a team of really hard, incredible newsmen with films, writing so-and-so-and-so-and-so-and-so. So that on the night of the show, in between all our songs is news, but the fastest and the hottest from every corner of the earth. And – dah-dah-dah – 'There's been an earthquake': just, like, incredible news in between each thing. So it's like a red hot news programme. And at the end, the final bulletin is… 'The Beatles Have Broken Up!'

John: I mean, I'm not going to lie, you know, I would sacrifice you all for her. This is how it was, you know. And that's all it was, though… She comes everywhere, you know.

Paul: So where's George?

John: Fuck knows where George is.

Yoko: Oh you can get back George so easily, you know that.

John: But it's not that easy because it's a festering wound that's been allowed to… and yesterday we allowed it to go even deeper, and we didn't give him any bandages.

Paul: See, I'm just assuming he's coming back, you know. I'm assuming he's coming back.

John: Well, do you…

Paul: If he isn't, then he isn't; then it's a new problem.

John: If we want him – I'm still not sure whether I do want him – but if we do decide we want him as a policy, I can go along with that because the policy has kept us together.

John and Paul lead a long conversation about George and the band's musical tensions, which also involves Ringo, Yoko and Linda.

John: It's like George said he didn't get enough satisfaction any more because of the compromise he had to make to be together [in The Beatles]… When something came out like *Revolver*, or whatever, there was still that element of surprise that we didn't know where it came from. But now we know exactly where it came from, and how it arrived at that particular noise, and how it could have been much better… or it needn't have been at all. The only way to get it satisfactory for yourself is to do it on your own, and then that's too hard.

Linda: But you were saying yesterday, you know… You make good music together, whether you like it or not.

John: I like it.

Linda: And making good music is also…

John: But it's just…

Linda: It's really hard working in a relationship.

John: I know.

A few moments later…

John: I'm too frightened to say, 'This is it,' but I'll just sit there and say, 'If you don't come along and play your bit, I won't do the song,' you know. I can't do any better than that. Don't ask me for what boogie you're going to play on this, 'cos, apart from not knowing, I can't tell you better than you – what you can play on it, you know. I can't do it like that. I never could, you know. Now when you think back on the other albums… I've never told you what to sing or what to play.

Paul: Yeah.

John: You know, I've always done the numbers like that. Now the only regret about the past numbers is when, because I've been so frightened, I've allowed you to take it somewhere I didn't want…

Paul: Yeah.

John: … and then that my only chance was to let George take over, or interest George in it, because I knew he'd…

Paul: 'She Said She Said'…

John: 'She Said She Said'.

Paul: I've never said to George, 'Look, George, I think when I want a guitar bit, I want it exactly like that one.' And he's going to say to me then, 'Well, you can't have it,' you know. See, but that's it. While he'd never say that to me, and I'd never say that to him, we go on and we get a problem. But really, it's going to be much better if we can actually just speak to one another and say, 'Look, George, on "I've Got A Feeling" I want you to do it exactly like me on bass…' and he'll say, 'Fuck you! And I can't do it exactly like you do it…'

John, Paul and Ringo work on 'Get Back'. Some time later…

Michael: I had a call from the facilities people who say that Denis [O'Dell] has cancelled all the stuff for the show. Do you think that's a good idea or not?

Mal: Do you want me to check it with him?

Paul: Yeah, I think so…

Michael: Well, just generally all the dates that we were talking about and everything.

Paul: Yeah, I think the 18th should be cancelled. I think…

Michael: Shall we make… try and make it a week later?

Paul: You see, the trouble is we're going to have to be, like…

Michael: You know, it's hard to talk about it.

Paul: Okay, so we have to be flexible, but we're going to have to be *very* flexible now, which is, like, the 18th today has changed to the 19th, 'cos we've lost a day today. Tomorrow it will change to the 20th. The day after it'll change to the 21st. Now if George comes…

Michael: Why not put it back for a week?

Paul: Well, exactly. If George comes back – yeah – put it back a full week, yeah.

Michael: Put it back a full week,

but book it for a full week, knowing that we can cancel it next week.

Paul: Yes.

Michael: If we can do that. We may have to pay a little bread and butter just to keep that going.

Paul: Okay.

Michael: I just – I mean, I don't… I think we should stay as flexible as we can.

Mal: In case we stay here.

Laughing.

John: [in West Country accent] Been more flexible before, Michael, I can tell you that.

Paul: Never been so flexible in my life.

Michael: Not to say changeable.

Paul: Yeah.

John: Well, I don't know if my favourite guitar here is a sign.

Paul: I'm leaving my ancient old Hofner. Look, look, what greater faith could man have than to leave his list?

Paul points out the set list taped to his bass, left there from The Beatles' final tour in 1966.

John: [sings in a crooner voice] 'No other love have I…'

Paul: [reads from list] 'She's a Woman', 'If I Needed [Someone]', '[Day] Tripper'…

Michael: What's it from?

John: That's from the old shows.

Michael: Oh, can we get a shot of this, Les?

John: [American accent] Yeah, Les, Les…

Paul: I wanna shot of this, Les. 'Baby's In Black'. 'If I Needed', 'Tripper', 'I Feel Fine', 'Yesterday'… 'I Wanna Be [Your Man]', 'Nowhere Man', 'Paperback [Writer]', 'Long Tall [Sally]'.

Michael: I think at some point we should talk conceptually about the show.

Everyone prepares to leave. A few moments later…

Michael: Bye, guys. See you, er…

Paul: Cheers.

Michael: … tomorrow.

Ringo: Good night, everybody.

Michael: What time? Ten?

Paul: Yeah.

Michael: Ten o'clock?

Paul: Yeah. Ten o'clock.

Michael: Ten o'clock.

Paul: Thinks – eleven.

Glyn: Thinks – twelve.

George remains absent. Paul is the first to show up, followed by Ringo. John and Yoko arrive some time later, and sit for an interview with Canadian Television. When it has finished, John begins mock-interviewing Paul…

John: [posh accent] Now we were going to discuss this afternoon, what religion meant to a pop star. And the pop star we've chosen is Ringo McCartney. Tell me, McCartney, does religion mean much to you in this present day, with all the trends and the swinging miniskirts that are about?
Paul: [Cockney accent] Fuck all!
John: Well, I can see that…
Paul: Fuck all!
John: … he's been disillusioned by the church in general in his remark of 'fuck all'.
Paul: No, well, I went to, er, Brighton with the, er, Maharishi. Fuck all, it meant to me!
John: Er, it was an important step for you?
Paul: Nothing. Nothing.
John: Er…
Paul: He didn't groove me.
John: He didn't groove?
Paul: No.
John: I see. I don't suppose he smoked pot, did he, by any…?
Paul: No!

John: I see. What about the Reverend Nipples?
Paul: No, not a chance.
John: Not a chance. Well, do you like, er, 'X' films?
Paul: Yep, yeah! Lulu, Barry Ryan and 'X' films. But Maharishi? No!
John: Well, I'd say that was a pretty concisive [*sic*] opinion of the youth of today. Now we're going on to a rather different group – er, generation gap – and that's Tumble Starker, who's sitting here. Now what do you think about mock Tudor shithouses in Weybridge, and places like that?
Yoko laughs.
Ringo: [posh accent] Well, I don't mind them being in Weybridge. It's just when they try and put them in London I think they get in the way of all the traffic. You're so right, yes.
John: As you said yesterday, 'Neither your arse, nor your elbow.'
Ringo: Nor your elbow; I said that.
Laughing.
John: I couldn't… I'll never forget it. Well, that's all for this evening. [hums a made-up theme tune]

While The Beatles are working at Twickenham, casting sessions are taking place for The Magic Christian, *which will star Ringo and Peter Sellers, and is being produced by Denis O'Dell. Enter Peter Sellers and Denis O'Dell, and Joe McGrath, director of* The Magic Christian, *who also shot The Beatles' promotional films for 'Day Tripper' and 'We Can Work It Out'. Peter and Joe soon sit next to John, Yoko, Paul, Ringo and Michael, watched by Mal and Glyn.*

John: Good evening.

Denis: We've got some more casting to do this afternoon, boys.

John: [to Peter Sellers] How are you?

Peter: All right, yeah.

John: Welcome to *Panorama*.

Peter: [to Yoko] Hello there.

Yoko: Hello.

Peter: How are you? Very pleased to meet you.

Paul: We need your help…

John: Pull up a star seat.

Paul: We'd like you to do a little introduction for *The Ed Sullivan Show*, Peter.

Laughing.

Peter: Oh ho, yeah. I'm very good at…

John: We've been lucky enough this evening to secure the, er, talents of Mr Peter Sellers here, who's going to give us Number 3.

Peter: Yes. Number 3, folks. Number 3.

John: How about that, folks? That was Number 3 from Peter Sellers. Now on to the next round.

Peter: Number 3, folks.

John: If we ask him really nicely, he'll probably do Number 5.

Peter: Yes, I might.

Laughing.

John: Over to you, Peter.

Paul: He is doing Number 5.

Peter: I can't count that far these days.

John: Never mind.

Peter: I used to be able to. [laughs]

Paul: Yes.

Peter: What are we…?

Paul: Well this is the… docu-mic.

John: It's a documentary of how The Beatles work.

Michael: It's a spontaneous documentary.

Paul: You meet everybody on film these days.

Peter: Oh really?

Laughing.

Paul: Just to keep them at their ease, you know.

John: We want to share with the world what, what we have, Peter, and this is what we have.

Yoko: Or what we haven't. [laughs]

John: We feel we shouldn't keep it all to ourselves. We should, s-spread it out, you know.

Peter: Yes, yes, yes, yes.

John: You know, do you?

Peter: In line with the, with the new thought, yes.

John: Oh yes.

Paul: Number 9.

Laughing.

Peter: I'm notoriously bad at this type of thing.

Paul: You've noticed, we are too. [laughs] It's half of the fun.

A few moments later…

Paul: You know, we just sort of put ourselves through the torture of being filmed…

Peter: It certainly is torture.

Paul: Having nothing to say and just sort of wiggling, nervously.

Ringo: Can we have some tea?

Paul: That's an idea, yeah.

Denis: Yeah, tea might be nice.

Paul: Can I have a tea, Mal?

John: Unaccustomed as I am to pubic hair…

Ringo: We'll have a tea party.

Mal: Who wants tea?

Peter: No, I need to be going.

Ringo: You want to go now, Peter?

Paul: This is the bit they always cut.

Peter: Very amusing.

John: It's the most exciting thing that's happened.

Michael: 'Cos otherwise we'd be grinding slowly to a halt.

Yoko: There's no business like no business.

Michael: There's no business like show business, well, there's no business like grinding to a halt.

Some time later…

Michael: We were talking earlier…

John: About the space between us? *Laughing.*

Michael: About the gap between us. But about the documentary, which is grinding to a halt – how we do it.

John: Grinding to a halt? I think it's taking off!

Paul: [laughs] It's taking… Here we go!

John: 'Loop de loop'… as Frankie Vaughan once said, the one-legged wonder!

Laughing.

Michael: Ringo said that he thought we ought to just tell it like it is. That's what I thought. But Mal thought we oughtn't to tell it like it is.

Paul: I think we are.

Towards the end of the day, John leads Paul and Ringo through an apparently unfinished new song.

John: [sings] 'Well there's a madman a-coming, gonna do you no harm/ He's wearing pink pyjamas and he lives on a farm/ He's gonna get you/ Got to get to somewhere to be alone/ Well, it's alright… Well, there's a fat freak who's coming, gonna feed you no shit/ It's gonna pull together/ Gonna give you some fit… Fifteen raw potatoes standing all in a row/ Don't you try to count 'em/ You just got it to go/ You've got to get somewhere/ To be so glad to be on your own/ And nowhere to go/ Nowhere to go/ Because you're going alone/ Nowhere to go because you're feelin' alone/ Feelin' alone/ Go home…'

THURSDAY
16 JANUARY
1969

Paul is the only Beatle present, along with Michael Lindsay-Hogg, Glyn Johns, Mal Evans, Denis O'Dell and Tony Richmond. He plays 'Oh! Darling' solo, at the piano. Shooting finishes early, and ends with the set being dismantled.

ACT TWO:
APPLE STUDIOS

21–31 JANUARY 1969

JOHN HARRIS

In the wake of George's sudden departure from Twickenham, two band meetings and a six-day break, The Beatles reunite and relocate to the basement of Apple's offices on Savile Row, in the West End of London. At George's behest, ideas of a climactic performance in front of an audience are sidelined, and the group concentrate instead on using their new songs for an album. On Monday 13 January, a deputation including Mal Evans and Glyn Johns is due to fly to Libya to take a close look at the amphitheatre, but the day after George's exit, as Mal puts it, The Beatles finally give up 'all idea of doing the TV show', and the trip is cancelled.

Nonetheless, Paul is clearly still attached to some kind of performance with an audience, an idea which will still come up in conversation, partly because Michael Lindsay-Hogg is keen for one to happen. Meanwhile, there is a big creative and emotional upswing, symbolised by the new song 'Get Back' decisively taking shape, and becoming – as the advert for its release as a single will put it – 'a song to roller-coast by'.

The new Apple studio is supposed to have been fitted out with equipment designed and built by The Beatles' friend 'Magic' Alex Mardas, the head of Apple Electronics, but what he has put in place is completely unusable. 'The mixing console was made of bits of wood and an old oscilloscope,' EMI engineer Dave Harries will recall. 'It looked like the control panel of a B-52 bomber.' In its place, George Martin – who, having been in the background at Twickenham, becomes a more noticeable presence at the sessions – arranges for recording equipment to be borrowed from Abbey Road, so The Beatles can work on releasable takes of their new songs. The Nagra tape recorders that have so far captured hours of conversation continue to do so.

A new face at the sessions is Billy Preston, a keyboard player The Beatles first met in Hamburg in 1962. Having recently seen him play alongside Ray Charles at the Royal Festival Hall, George invites him to the basement, and Billy then

plays a central role right until the end of the sessions. The Beatles' organisation finds him a flat in Chelsea, and the band begin to make plans for Billy's future releases as an Apple recording artist.

Throughout the time they spend at Apple (which includes a weekend), they not only record the songs that eventually appear on the *Let It Be* album, but also work on material that will end up on the album *Abbey Road* – which is not, as commonly thought, a record whose creativity and invention represents *Let It Be*'s opposite, but one that actually grows organically out of these increasingly productive sessions. But there are also signs of looming discord. On the evening of 27 January, John and Yoko have their first meeting with Allen Klein, the American businessman whose presence at the heart of The Beatles' affairs will play a key role in the band's break-up. Less dramatically, the question of how to bring the sessions to a close and give Michael Lindsay-Hogg the kind of finale he requires remains unresolved. A solution, it eventually transpires, lies four storeys above…

TUESDAY
21 JANUARY
1969

A short day. George's return is not mentioned on the tapes. As the band and everyone working on the film arrive, the studio is still being set up.

Michael: Not bad, though. I mean, you've done it very quickly.

Mal: Oh it's not bad. Much nicer than any other studio.

Ringo: It was lovely walking in here yesterday after Twickenham.

Mal: Yeah, right.

Ringo: It really was.

Mal: It's a bit of calm, you know.

Michael: In retrospect I'm glad we got out.

Mal: Yeah.

Michael: There was something queer about Twickenham. I don't know what it was.

Ringo: Too big.

Michael: Too big.

Ringo: For what we were doing, you know. And this is nicer.

Eventually, John, Yoko, Michael and Glyn discuss The Rolling Stones Rock And Roll Circus, *and the need for John to film a brief link for it.*

Michael: [to John] If we have time and it makes sense to shoot it, would you like to do the link into the Stones for the Circus? Or would you not like that?

John: Well, well, what kind of thing?

Michael: It could just be, 'And now ladies and gentlemen, your host for this evening – The Rolling Stones', or words to that effect.

John: If it's straight then I'll do it.

Michael: Yeah, it's straight.

John: Can we just do it in the other room, or something?

Michael: Yeah, let's do it as a big close-up.

John: I was watching the bits we shot last night, you know.

Michael: Mmm. Mmm.

John: Looked all right.

Michael: Your number's going to be great. We saw the rough cut last night, which is looking good…

What I haven't cut well yet is your number, or 'Sympathy [For The Devil]'. *A few moments later.*

John: While we were making the Stones' show we had these people from Austria [who were also working on John and Yoko's film *Rape*] filming us there. So when we were on stage, or Marianne Faithfull was singing her number, our guys were just sort of picking it up on a mic. [mimics Marianne Faithfull] She's a bit like Edith Piaf.

Michael: Yeah, yeah.

George, John, Yoko, Ringo and Derek Taylor, Apple's head of press, discuss the Daily Sketch*'s account of George leaving the filming at Twickenham, written by the journalist Michael Housego.*

John [to Derek]: Have you seen Michael Housego today? Don't you think it's suable?

Derek: No.

John: What, about the fisticuffs?

Derek: He said it didn't take place.

John: He said it did, didn't he?

Derek: No.

George: Yes he did.

Ringo: He said it might of [*sic*].

John: Yes, in the past. Well, that's false too. It's never got to that, except for a plate of dinner in Hamburg… [referring to the report, and laughing] George Harrison, the sane one, speaks out.

Enter Paul, who picks up a copy of The Rolling Stones' Beggars Banquet, closely reading what's on the sleeve. George looks through several other albums, including Smokey Robinson and The Miracles' Make It Happen and Greatest Hits. They work on 'Dig A Pony', punctuated by Paul briefly playing 'Every Night' (which will appear on his first solo album), and a run of busked songs including 'Run For Your Life', Tommy Tucker's 1964 hit 'Hi-Heel Sneakers', 'My Baby Left Me' and 'That's All Right (Mama)' (both made famous by Elvis), and Chuck Berry's 'Little Queenie'.

Paul: [reading from report in a blank, nasal voice, and adding his own satirical touches] 'The awful tension of being locked in each other's arms snapped last night at a TV rehearsal, and Beatles John, George, Paul and Harold … at the very least, a few vicious phrases took place … It is only the suddenness of their decline from the status of "boys next door" to the category of "weirdies" that has left most people agog … It would be about the middle of 1966 that the personal lustre of The Beatles began to show a few spots of rust. I will deliberately leave Ringo out of it because he has never developed an inclination towards the bizarre. Lennon was married, happily, McCartney was going steady, and George Harrison was about to marry. Everything in the Beatle

garden was rosy. But that was a long time [ago]…'
John: [sings] 'Early in the morning/ I'm a-givin' you the warning/ Don't you step on my blue suede shoes…'
Paul: [continues reading] '… Whatever talent they have as individuals – and who can deny it – their capacity to earn is largely tied up in their performances as a group.'
John: [sings] 'You got nothing to lose/ You got nothing to hide/ No no, you got nothing inside…'
Paul: [continues reading] 'Until they are either rich enough for that not to matter or fed up enough that they'll stay together…'
John: [sings] 'Early in the morning/ I'm a-givin' you the warning/ [Don't] You step on my blue suede shoes…'
Paul: [continues reading] '… because of the economic necessity. But I can't say definitely that as the friendly foursome tied irrevocably to each other's pigtails, it's all over. They will never be exactly the same again.'
John: [sings] 'Well I heard the news/ Everybody's rockin' tonight…'

Work on 'Dig A Pony' is followed by a brief snatch of 'I've Got A Feeling'.
John: Let's record as many as we know.
Paul: Okay.
John: We'll do that, then 'I've Got A Feeling', then 'Don't Let Me Down',

and best of luck on that middle bit.
Paul: [posh accent] Okay. That sounds fair enough.
John: Sounds fairy queen. San Fairy Ann.
Paul: [American accent] San Fairy Ann Francisco.
After more work on 'Dig A Pony'…
John: Ha! It's getting better.
Paul: [Scottish accent] Got to admit it's getting worse.
John: Aye!

They work on 'I've Got A Feeling' and 'Don't Let Me Down', before listening to playbacks of 'I've Got A Feeling' and 'Dig A Pony'. Some time later…
Paul: [reading list, in comical Northern accent] 'All I Want Is You' [i.e 'Dig A Pony'], 'The Long And Winding Road', 'Bathroom Window', 'Let It Be'…
George: … 'Bathroom Window'.
Paul: … 'Across The Universe', 'Get Back To Where You Once Belonged', 'Two Of Us On Our Way Home', 'Maxwell's Silver Hammer', 'I've Got A Feeling', 'Sunrise', 'I Me Mine'.
George: 'Sunrise'?
Paul: Er… 'All Things Must Pass'.
John: [in similar comic accent] You threw me there. I thought, 'I was away a day. They learnt a fucking tune! They learnt a fucking tune!'
They work on 'She Came In Through The Bathroom Window', before the day reaches its end.

***WEDNESDAY
22 JANUARY
1969***

The first day with Billy Preston on keyboards. Paul, Michael Lindsay-Hogg and Tony Richmond are talking about the show.

Michael: Shall we say we'll do it this weekend week [i.e. in ten days' time]? Because I think we ought to set us a time.

Paul: Sure. Yeah. Or maybe we don't need to do it on a weekend.

Michael: We can do it on a weekday.

Paul: Maybe.

Michael: Shall we say we'll do it a week from tomorrow? 'Cos you see… we ought to get together. If we're going to have it out of doors, whether people just turn up or what they do, let's kind of get a little organisation here.

Tony: Well, if you do it at Primrose Hill or somewhere like that, people are going to turn up, you know.

Michael: Yeah.

Tony: You're going to get kids and everybody.

Michael: We also have to get the gear together, though.

Tony: Yeah. Do you want to do it on film or [video] tapes, Paul?

Paul: I don't mind. I don't care. I really don't. You know, you get the picture, you get what you wanted originally.

Michael: What I'd like to do is go and talk to Neil about seeing if Primrose Hill

is free. Can I do that? I can do that.

Paul: Sure. It would be nice almost not to tell 'em. So it's better not to tell 'em, just to sort of…

Tony: Well, we could get that together, and suddenly just one day we say, 'Right, we're going to Primrose Hill.'

Paul: You know, and then turn it into a TV show… I thought about it last night – the LA idea where we were just going to turn up and all the groups were going to appear. Because Primrose Hill, you know, people really would [come]… And the police would come, and where do you get enough lads [i.e officers], you know.

Michael: That's what I want to do in Africa, where you just start playing – and one by one they come, one by one, ten by ten, twenty…

Tony: To do it in the week would be much better, 'cos you get…

Paul: Yeah, you'll get all the week people.

Tony: Because you get the week people, the mothers and the kids and the nurses and their dogs…

Paul: Which is much more a scene on Primrose Hill.

Michael: Yeah, great. But the only thing is, we've – we've got to get…

Paul: What's that? [giggles]

Michael: We've got to get some permission, Paul… so the cops don't

come and throw us off, that's all.

Tony: You get that from the park.

Paul: Yes, yes, yes. I like the idea of just doing it… And again, you see, you've got to make it easy on yourself, I suppose. Once we get it into anything, everyone's going to disagree… if the night after we've done [a run-through] here, we could just say, 'How about tomorrow?' 'Cos everyone felt so good, the people'd say, 'What? Do what?' 'Just play it all for ourselves now that we've rehearsed.' And then really just sort of do it like that.

Michael: Right.

Paul: Imagine if we could possibly turn up anywhere… you know, just go to Primrose Hill… Get in the vans, you know, get a big outside broadcast team together, to shoot… like they cover racing.

Tony: Then you just have to choose within a few days.

Michael: Good. But just roughly time-wise so I can look into gear – you say in about a week?

Paul: Yeah. A week from this weekend probably is likely. But, you know…

Tony: Okay.

Paul: Maybe not. When do you think we'll be ready to do it? [chuckles]

Michael: How long would you like – about another ten days?

Enter George.
George: But are you still trying to do it with [an] audience, all in one go?
Michael: It's still open.
George: If we're just trying to make the album, I think we should just start it straight away… Are we going to do it all here now?
Paul: I think so, yeah.
George: Or was this just rehearsing until EMI was opened?
Michael: I think we can do it here and get people into here. I think whatever we do we ought to get people in, 'cos that changes the character of the piece.
Paul: So okay, look, if we say, say, a week on Friday or something, you know. Then it'll be pretty quick but it'll still give us some time to do it.

Some time later…
John: [to Paul] Did you see Fleetwood Mac on *Late Night Live*?
Paul: See what?
John: Fleetwood Mac on *Late Night Live*. Oh, they were so sweet, man.
Paul: Were they?
John: And the lead singer's great, you know… Just very quiet, they play. But just so sweet. And they do that old, rock'n'roll sort of drumming, or early blues drumming, you know – like brushes: 'tch tch tch tch tch'. It's just very quiet and he sings very quiet as well. He's not a shouter…
Paul: It's a bit like the Canned Heat thing.
John: Yeah, but better than Canned Heat.
George: There was only four of them last night, wasn't there?
John: Yeah. They're really good, though, aren't they?
They work on 'Dig A Pony'.
Sandwiches arrive.
Glyn: Oooo, sarnies. That's good news.
Whistling.
John: Okay lads, let's bang it.
Glyn: Sandwiches. I'm bloody starving! May I?
John: Er, I'd like the Fleetwood Mac album for my lunch.

After working on 'Dig A Pony', they turn to 'I've Got A Feeling'. During the outro, John begins improvising.
John: I had a dream this afternoon…
Paul: Yeah, I had a dream…
John: I had a dream this afternoon…
Paul: Well, I had a dream… When all the people…
The music stops.
Paul: … shall be united.
John: Did you hear Martin Luther King? Fantastic! No wonder they shot him… [shouts] 'I had a dream this afternoon, children. I dreamt the black and the white kids are gonna be together.'
Paul: '… Walk together, hand in hand.'
John: Like a big poem, it was… No wonder they got him, you know… He would have been President, you know. He was fantastic. Just like a poem.
Michael: And his voice was like a singer's.
Yoko: He should have been the President of the United States.
John: Yeah. Fantastic, you know.
Paul: When did he get shot, then? Was it like that…?
John: About a year or two ago. After [President] Kennedy.
Paul: … And some nut too, you know, some white nut.
John: But it's not nuts, man. It's business.
Paul: Yeah.
John: It's business.

Enter Billy Preston. All four Beatles gather round him, evidently thrilled by his arrival.
Billy: How you doing? Hello, Ringo.
Ringo: How you doing, baby? Good to see you.
Billy: How you doing, Ringo? Good to see you, mate. Outta sight, man.
Laughter.
George: How's your show?
Billy: Fantastic.
John: Pull up a wire…
Paul: Sit down.
John: Here y'are.

A few moments later.
George: [to Billy] What happened to [Little] Richard?
Billy: He's still travelling around doing his thing.
George: Where is he?
John: Is he with [singer] Larry Williams?
Billy: Yes.
John: They're nearly getting it, but not hitting it…
Billy: No… He's having a rough time now.
George: Is he in LA?
Billy: He told me he was coming here.
George: 'Cos I asked everybody in LA I knew if they knew where Richard was, but nobody knew.
Billy: No. 'Cos he's kinda hard to find, you know… all over… everywhere.
John: He's just trying to be hip all the time.
Billy: Yeah.

After stopping, the tape starts again.
John: [to Billy]… straight off, one number after the other. And that means having somebody in on the scene. So if you'd like to do that, you're welcome.
Billy: Sure. Beautiful.
Paul: Do you wanna session, John?
John: Right. And then you'd be on the album, you know.
Billy: You're kidding. [laughs]
John: That'd be your first release, on the album.
Paul: [laughing] Yeah.
John: 'Cos every number's got a piano part… and normally we overdub it, you know.
Billy: Uh-huh.
John: But this time we want to do it live.
Billy: Yeah.
John: We've taped a few; the thing is to get some tapes made of what we've done and then he'll have a listen – take them home at night.
George: He'll probably just pick 'em up much quicker here, you know, just hearing 'em.
John: Yeah.
Paul: Just rehearsing.

RAY CHARLES ORCHESTRA
AUSTRALIA
AUGUST 1967

They play 'I've Got A Feeling', which Billy soon joins in on, before moving on to 'Dig A Pony'. Then…

John: Okay. 'Don't Let Me Down', Billy. Change of atmosphere. All the chords are E and F-sharp-minor all the time.

Billy: Right.

John: F-sharp-minor goes [plays chord]…

Billy plays the chord on the organ.

John: What's that?

Paul: Let's hear it again.

Billy: I can hear it.

John: Yeah. You can hear it. And then it just hits B for a minute at one point.

Billy: I've got perfect pitch.

John laughs. The song starts. Billy soon adds an electric piano solo.

John: 'Can you dig it?'

Paul: [sings] 'Woo-woo…'

John: [shouts] I had a dream this afternoon… Don't let me down…

They continue playing 'Don't Let Me Down'.

John: [animatedly] It's great. You say, 'Take it,' and he takes it. You're giving us a lift, Bill.

Billy: Oh, really?

John: We've been doing this for days, you know.

Paul: Weeks.

John: [to George Martin] Have you met Billy, George?

George Martin: How do you do, Billy.

John: That's George Martin, our A&R man. That's Billy, he plays for Ray Charles. Also, we played with him in Hamburg. He was backing Little Richard in Hamburg.

Billy: Yes.

Paul: In the old days.

Some time later, as they listen to playbacks in the just-built control room…

George: I feel much better since Billy came, because I feel as though he's doing fills which…

Paul: That we should have been doing, yeah.

George: 'Cos sometimes it's like… any time there's a space missing, it's as if, 'Oh, fuck, I'm not filling that space

again.' But, you know, it works out much better.

John: And it's better in 'Dig A Pony' too, you know…

George: Yeah.

John: I don't have to worry about my rhythm, really.

Paul: Yeah, it's great.

Michael: Is he going to stay with you?

John: Yeah. He's the guy. And that solves a lot, you know… Paul was like, we do the whole show once here, and then maybe do it up Primrose Hill or something, you know…

Michael: What I think we can do is do it here. Do it here and then, like, take it…

John: Yeah. Or otherwise we could do half of the LP here, and the other half outside, you know.

Michael: I think what we should do is probably do it all here and not outside.

John: It'll be fantastic with this whole build-up with bits of paper, and

Twickenham, and all that scene, and, you know… it's like getting Wordsworth or something, [writing] from the start. Instead of having to get an actor to go through the bits, and re-enact his life… It'll be marvellous. And it'll be a movie, you know, not a TV show. It'll be the third Beatles movie.

Allan Williams, the Liverpool promoter who arranged their first dates in Hamburg, watches as they play 'Don't Let Me Down' again, followed by 'I've Got A Feeling'.

John: See you tomorrow, then.

Michael: What time are you cats coming in? About ten?

Paul: The cats are coming in at eleven.

Michael: Eleven or twelve.

Paul: Good night, Mr Williams.

Michael: Okay.

Paul: See you tomorrow.

Michael: See you tomorrow. Don't worry. Everything's fine.

THURSDAY
23 JANUARY
1969

The Beatles are eating breakfast and discussing their progress with Glyn and George Martin, while Ringo works on 'Octopus's Garden' at the piano.

Ringo: Aaarrgh! [Work] this weekend, then you have three weekends off.
George Martin: Yeah. Why not work this weekend, John?
Glyn: That would be the answer to all, wouldn't it?
Yoko: This weekend? Ohhh!
Ringo: You know, if we did ten days straight from now, we should…
Yoko: Okay. Ten…
George Martin: I mean, you're working so well together now…
John: Yes.
George Martin: Let's keep it going.
John: Well, you know, I won't say no.
Some time later…
John: [to Paul] Michael was talking in terms of [a show] next Thursday…
Paul: Yes.
John: And working over the weekend.
George: Was he now?
John: So… it's going to be stupid.
Paul: Ah. Yeah. Let's work Saturday, but not Sunday. Just to have one day, 'cos it does help next week…
John: [coughs] Oh yeah.
Paul: … if we get one [extra] day.
A moment later…
Paul: Let's do 'Get Back', 'cos we were getting into good things…

'Get Back' is now taking shape. Joined again by Billy Preston, the band work on its arrangement, and lyrics. They play the first verse, about Jo Jo, from Tucson, Arizona.

Paul: I like the words of that verse now. It's something about he knew he was a loner, but… He *thought* he was a loner, but he…
John: Knew it couldn't last.
Paul: Yeah, but he knew it couldn't last, so he left his home in Tucson, Arizona… There's this ranch, in Tucson, Arizona. It's in the mountains, and it's a cattle ranch. It's an incredible place apparently, and just near the border into Mexico – between Mexico and Tucson –

and, er, we got it…
John: Are you buying it?
Paul: No. We've got it for May. These people who own it don't use it in May.
Ringo suddenly finds the beat that will define the finished version.
Paul: 'Get back, get back, Jo Jo, get back, get back to where you once belonged/ There's a pretty woman waitin' on the corner for you, Jo Jo/ Wearing high heel shoes/ There's a pretty woman with her high heel shoes and her bright pink lipstick, Jo Jo/ Get back to Tucson…'
More work on the song.
Paul: I just have the story about Sweet Loretta Martin.
John: Oh yeah. [clears throat]
Paul: [sings] 'Sweet Loretta Martin thought she was a woman…' John – what have you got?
John: What?
Paul: But then… the story about Loretta; and then Jo Jo, who thought he was a loner and goes to California for some grass. But then it's like at the end…
He plays a snatch.
Paul: [sings] 'Get back, get back, Jo Jo/ Get back to Sweet Loretta/ He's waitin' for you [laughs]'… [speaking] With his old drag queen back on the ranch… 'Wearing his high heel shoes/ Get back, Jo Jo, to where you once belonged…'
More rehearsal of 'Get Back'.
Paul: Is that coffee?
George: It's a teabag, and it's got slime on it.
John: [in a nasal, camp voice] I've ordered some nice tea from a health shop, Paul. It'll be very nice later on.
A few moments later…
John: Let's have one guitar solo and one piano solo.
Paul: Okay.
John: Because I'll only be able to work one out.
Paul: Who do you want to be? Jo Jo or Loretta?
Laughing.
Paul: Let's see who we are when it comes up.
John: Okay.

They rehearse 'Get Back' into the afternoon, and also play 'Oh! Darling', after which Billy plays songs – including four that will end up on his future solo albums, on Apple Records – at the piano. Then John and Paul (on drums) jam with Yoko on a fierce, feedback-laden improvisation, which lasts around ten minutes, before George, Ringo and Billy take their places.

John: I think we just made an LP. [to George] You missed it.

George: Oh!

John: Ray Charles was here.

George: The lights are working.

John: They were, they just went off. We blew it.

Yoko: Just went off. [laughs]

John: [enthusiastically] It was great. Did it… was it all on film?

Michael: Yeah.

John: What a great bit of film that was – just *kkkhhhhh*…

Yoko: [laughs] It was… it was good. *Background chat.*

Paul: I think you're nuts, the pair of you.

John: Yeah.

They return to working on 'Get Back'. With Glyn and Denis, everyone then listens to a playback.

John: Can we have this morning's?

Paul: Yeah. It was better this morning.

Everyone talks at once.

Paul: But they [i.e. songs] do that, you know. They go through the good bit then the bad, and then…

John: It's just this morning we first hit on that slow beat…

George: It'd be nice to just work that one, you know, just do takes until we get it, and before the show, just put it out as a single.

John: Yeah.

George: Just do a single of it, now, you know.

John: Okay, let's knock it off for a single, then.

Paul: Pardon?

John: Let's finish it off for a single tomorrow.

George: Do you want to just make it now, and we'll have it as a single and put it out next week?

Paul: Oh yeah.

Ringo: Yeah.

John: And we'll do Part Two on the back [*sic*] side…

George: Yeah.

John: … with Billy and us just *loco*.

Glyn: Just an instrument duel?

John: [enthusiastically] Yeah.

George: Do it, then.

Paul: [in Scouse accent] Oh, I'm easy, like.

**FRIDAY
24 JANUARY
1969**

John, Yoko, Paul and George are having breakfast. Billy Preston is elsewhere. Enter Ringo.

John: [to Ringo] Hello, Richard.
Ringo: Hello, John.
Yoko: I'm trying [the toast] without the marmalade today, you know.
John: Very good.
Yoko: Ah…
John: You see what happens.
Yoko laughs.
John: Bad karma.
Laughing.
George: It's funny, isn't it? I keep thinking any minute the whistle'll go and we'll all have to go into Assembly or something.

Michael talks to John about his appearance in The Rolling Stones Rock And Roll Circus *('I was doing a bit of "Yer Blues" this morning – it's looking very good'), before all four Beatles talk about Billy Preston: his work on the sessions, and plans for his solo releases on Apple.*
George: Billy just really is so knocked out, so thrilled [to be] doing it. And also, you know, he sees it as a

great opportunity…
John: Yeah. I see it as ours too.
George: You know, I mean, he could be…
John: Yeah, like a fifth Beatle.
George: We could have him in The Beatles as well.
John: I'd like a fifth Beatle.
Paul: I just don't. Because it's just bad enough with four… [smiling] It's creating havoc, you know… I dig him. He's an incredible musician, you know…

The band work on 'Two Of Us', which is now slower than the Twickenham version, but still based on the same feel. It then quickly acquires the arrangement used on the finished version, which Paul compares to 'I'll Follow The Sun' from Beatles For Sale.
Paul: It's like, after 'Get Back' – 'We're on our way home'.
John: Yeah.
Paul: So there's a story. And there's another one – 'Don't Let Me Down'. [sings] 'Oh! Darlin' I'll never let you down…'
John: Yeah. It's like you and me are lovers.

Paul: Yeah.
John: We shall have to camp it up for those two.
Paul: Yeah, well, I'll be wearing my skirt on the show anyway.
More work on the song.
George: Shall we hear it?
Eager panting.
John: [making his way to the control room] Track it. Put the violins on. Let's go.
George: Put it on the B-side [of 'Get Back'].
Paul: Release it.
John: Release it in Italy only. Let's just make a different single for every country… Just every song we make we release as a single somewhere. Because every one suits one country.
George: It sounds lovely that, now. After all the anguish we went through with it.
John: Well, it's part of the, the pudding… It's a Henry Moore sculpture, that.
George Martin: And the fact that you're working so well together: you're looking at each other, you're seeing each other, you're… just *happening*. [clicks fingers]

Paul introduces the band to his new song 'Teddy Boy', which John accompanies with mock instructions for a square dance: 'Take your partners and do-si-do/ Hold them tight and don't let go/ When you've got it, jump up/ And take your partners and do-si-do/ And when you've got it then let it go.' They return to 'Two Of Us'. John then leads the rendition of 'Maggie Mae' that will appear on the Let It Be *album. They soon break for lunch, preceded by Mal writing down what everyone wants.*

George: [to Mal] Have you got any Japanese mushrooms?

Mal: Yeah, mushroom soup.

John: Have you got any rice? Brown rice, can I have? Well, get 'em to get it in, will you, Doris. Okay?

Ringo: Mashed potato.

John: Don't do it, Richie. Don't do it.

Paul: Are you doing anything?

John: I was going to have rice and vegetables.

Yoko: No, we have mushrooms [and] vegetables, then.

Mal: Does it have to be brown rice?

John: Yeah, it's got to be brown rice. The other's shit, you know.

Yoko: Because the other rice is sticky… We'll have omelettes, then, you know.

George: What sort of vegetables do you like?

John: Oh, all of them, you know – cauliflower… carrots…

George: We'll have whatever the vegetables are, if they've got any cheese sauce for the cauliflower.

Yoko: … just mushrooms and vegetables…

John: Well, let's have a mushroom omelette, then, you know.

George: Well, you know, they seemed to give us cauliflower yesterday…

Yoko: Mushroom omelette…

John: It'll actually have it mixed in.

George: I'd like cheese sauce with the cauliflower.

John plays 'Polythene Pam'. Soon after, accompanied by the band, with John on the slide guitar he will later use on 'For You Blue', Paul plays snatches of 'Her Majesty', followed by a song about his Yorkshire Terrier, 'Eddie', never finished. John joins in. Paul then begins playing 'Every Night'. He also plays a snatch of 'Hot As Sun', written before The Beatles made it, and also destined for his debut solo album. The band once again work on 'Two Of Us', which turns into the '50s hit 'Singing The Blues'. Pattie Harrison arrives, just as John starts improvising over a blues jam, led by his lap-steel guitar.

John: [sings] 'Oh, hit it, man!'

Paul: Well…

John: Yeah. Oh, yeah, sing it! Can you dig it? Can you dig it? Can you dig it? Can you dig it? I can dig it. Can you dig it? Can you dig it? Can you dig it?

Paul: [singing] 'Can you dig it, yeah?'

John: Well, can you dig it?

Paul: Can you dig it, yeah?

John: Well, can you dig it?

Paul: I can dig it, yeah.

John: [sings] 'Yeah. Well can you…?/ Well can you dig it?/ Well can you dig it?/ Well can you dig it?/ Well you can dig it every mornin'/ Dig it every evenin'/ Dig it every time somebody gives it to you, boy/ Well can you dig it?/ Well can you dig it?/ Well can you dig it?/ Well can you dig it?/ Well you can dig it every mornin'/ Dig it every evenin'/ Dig it every time somebody gives it to you, boy…' … [in falsetto voice] That was Can You Dig It by Georgie Wood. And now we'd like to do Hark The Angels Come…

Paul: [sings in mock tremolo voice] 'Hark the angels come, oh my darling…' *Some time later…*

Paul: [in Scouse accent] It's seven o'clock, you know, John. Got to knock off.

John: Maisy and Daisy don't want to go.

Paul: Look, John, if you're prepared to pay us overtime…

**SATURDAY
25 JANUARY
1969**

Billy is once again elsewhere. The band listen to playbacks of 'Get Back', 'Teddy Boy', 'I've Got A Feeling', 'Two Of Us' and 'Dig A Pony'.

John: [on the tape] I cocked it up trying to get loud.
Paul: [on the tape] Yeah, I know…
John: [still on the tape] It's not bad, though.
Glyn: Beautiful. 'Not bad, though.' It's beautiful.
Laughing.
Glyn: It's all you need.
John: Oh, yeah, I know this.
Paul: Great, great, great.
The band work on 'Two Of Us', sung by John and Paul in a variety of comical accents.
John: [sings] 'I met her on a Monday and her head stood still/ Da doo ron ron ron/ Da do ron ron…'
Paul: Oh, I saw that film last night.
John: What?
Paul: Of us at the Maharishi's. I've got all the [home movie] film of it.

John: Oh yeah.
Paul: And all sort of together… incredible.
John: I've got a couple of reels of it at home…
Paul: It's just got a great opening.
John: The helicopter one up in the sky.
Paul: Yeah. I noticed you taking it [i.e. the helicopter], so I thought, I'll get that.
John: Well, that was the idea, you know, 'cos you said you were going to film it.
Paul: But it is great, it's incredible, you know… just [to] sort of see us, what we're doing. It's unbelievable.
George: What were you doing?
John: Yes, what *were* we doing?
Paul: Well, I don't really know, you know. But it's like we'd totally sort of put our own personalities under for the sake of it, and you can really see, you know, we're all, sort of…
John: Who's writing all them songs?
Paul: Oh, that was probably when we did an incredible number, you know. [regaining thread] But there's a long

shot of you walking…
George: Do you regret having gone there?
Paul: [emphatically] No, no. Oh no, no.
John: I don't regret anything… ever. Not even Bob Wooler.
Wooler was the Cavern Club DJ who John physically attacked in 1963, after he intimated John was romantically involved with Brian Epstein.
Paul: No, I just think… we weren't sort of really very truthful there, you know.… Things like sneaking behind his [i.e. the Maharishi's] back and sort of saying, 'It's a bit like school, isn't it?' But you can see on the film that it is very like school and that, really, we should have sort of *said*…
John: You want to call it 'What We Did On Our Holidays'.
Paul: There's a long shot of you sort of walking with him – and it's just not you, you know. [chuckles] It's just sort of, [in American accent] 'Tell me, O Master…'
John: 'Tell me, O Master…'
Paul: And Linda remembered that thing

you said the other night about when you went up in the helicopter with him. You just thought he might slip you the answer.

Laughing.

John: I thought he might fly off home.

Paul: 'Hey, John, by the way…'

John: '… I've been meaning to tell you…'

Paul: 'I've been meaning to tell you, son…'

John: 'The word is "vajira".'

Laughing.

George: I wouldn't mind having, er…

John: I wouldn't mind having his money.

Laughing.

George: I wouldn't mind having two months out of every four months in a place like that, though.

Paul: It's incredible stuff. And then the next scene burns out white again, and the next scene is just this monkey that just comes up and humps this other monkey.

Laughing.

Paul: It's great, you know. And I mean

the way, oh, he really gets up there – [he] really just stretches her out. And then they just jump off, and they just start sort of picking each other. Just jumping.

A few moments later…

Paul: It's that thing, you know: we probably should have sort of…

John: Been ourselves.

Paul: Yeah. A lot more, yeah.

George: That's like the biggest joke – 'to be yourselves'. 'Cos that was the purpose of going there, to try and find yourself.

John: Yeah. Well, we found that, didn't we?

George: And if you were really yourself you wouldn't be any of who we are now.

Paul: Mmm.

John: All act naturally, then.

John/Paul: [singing] 'They're gonna put me in the movies/ They're gonna make a big star out of me…'

John: We'd better do a few numbers, hadn't we… 'cos it's Wednesday.

*They carry on rehearsing 'Two Of Us',
before Ringo comes out from behind
his drums and they discuss how the film
might end, with Michael and Glyn.*

John: There isn't any big scene now –
all we've got is us, and the documentary,
where we happen to be singing. And
that bit [i.e. the show] has gone. I
thought that was all over, you know.

Paul: What?

John: The bit about the show, the
finale. The finale'd just be us doing the
numbers well.

Paul: Yeah. I think it probably is, yeah…

John: But lit as nicely as you can.

Paul: I dig a show, you know. I dig a
pony. I like that, and I always have, you
know.

John: Well… what are you trying to
make a show out of now?

Paul: I can't answer it, you know.

John: I know.

Paul: I know that there's no sort of
answer for it. But… I can't put it into
words. It's a bit like what's wrong with
Apple.

John: Too many people. [laughs]

Paul: I just like making the best out of
an idea – sort of grabbing the remnants
of an idea, making that into…

John: It's after the horse has gone,
you know. We started it like that, and
now we're salving [*sic*] it like that really,
aren't we?

Paul: Anyway, we'll decide later what it
turns into.

Michael: What was originally [the] idea,
was a show and a documentary… and
that went out the window.

John: Well, originally it was a show, and
then a show and a documentary, and
the show vanished.

Paul: But I'm making another album
again, you know. And I'd meant to put
them into some other framework this
time. That's what I sort of thought. And
the only one other thing was the TV
show, you know…I do like to get out
– get out in the open, have a change
of scene, and go and do it somewhere
else, do it on a live show, or do it even
[on] a TV studio floor, do it on a stage…
just without a sort of feeling of…

John: That's what the big thing was about. Nobody else wants to go on the stage or do a TV show, you know, that's what it's about. Nobody wants to get out there, you know. And then if you want to get out there, you'll have to find some other form of getting out there.

Paul: I suppose that's true, you know.

John: I think so, you know. I'm only going by what's happened.

Paul: Yeah, yeah.

John: [to George] What do you think? I mean that's what it was about, wasn't it?

George: That's why I can't… you know, it's being this funny thing about…

Glyn: What we've got is you all playing live in one room. This is it, right, for the first time, for a start, and it's really working extremely well. That in itself is a fresh thing for The Beatles.

George: You know, we've really wasted a lot of time, because we could have just worked out which number, and done it, and got it really good – and even good live – just like that.

John: Yeah. Had we chosen in the beginning to do this, though.

George: And we would have had about five tracks already.

Paul: I don't know why I'm moaning.

Michael: What you're moaning about is there's no payoff.

Glyn: Every idea that we could think of was put forward, and everybody tried to get it together, really… nobody could have tried harder, but it didn't happen. So if it didn't happen, so the time isn't right for that [laughs], so let's do this. And this is so good. This is great.

John: See, it's turned out [like] that, and it's not what Paul wants… Say it's his number, this whole show, well, he's compromised, so that it's actually turned into our number more than his number…

Paul: Yeah. And that's all right, you know.

John: It's all right. But that's what's bugging you really, 'cos it's a different number, you know. It's turned into a rock number or, as opposed to a quiet number or something like that. And… [pause]… it's just that, really.

Paul: But it's just funny to sort of realise that after this is all over, you'll be off in a black bag somewhere… [in] the Albert Hall, you know. And sort of doing shows and stuff, you know, and digging that thing a bit.

John: But I would dig to play on stage, you know. I mean, if everything was all right and there was no messing and we were just going to play on stage.

Paul: Yeah. But it's only that. It's only that. I'd like to see Ringo [playing]… and all that.

John: That's why I said yes to the TV show. [But] I didn't want the hell of doing it… I like playing. That's why I went on the Stones' show [the *Rock And Roll Circus*], you know, and that's why I'll do other things. But if we all don't want to do that…

Paul: Yeah, I know. It's like majority decisions.

John: But I don't want to sort of go on the road again.

A moment of silence, punctuated by George's guitar.

Paul: I just feel as though we *are* on the road again. We're in a studio, and we just keep to the same environment totally, always, you know. We don't ever attempt to break out of it.

Yoko: Maybe next week they might change their minds.

Paul: It's nicer in a warm climate, you know.

George: I think this is the nicest place I've been for a long time, this studio.

Paul: Yeah, it is.

George: And also, this is the most I've ever played by playing every day. And I can just feel my fingers getting loose a bit, you know, because we don't get the chance to do that. But if we go out on the road, then it gets back into that one. And really I just want to play. And you can play better without having to do all those things.

Paul: Yeah.

A few moments later…

Paul: I don't know what it is, you know, that I'm moaning about, but it's just sort of…

Glyn: I must admit I can't really see either because [laughs] it just seems the last two days, everything's gone so ridiculously well.

Paul: It is great. It's going great.

Yoko: Great. And maybe next week, you know, it might change. You don't know.

Paul: Yeah, sure.

Yoko: I mean, it might be great and maybe everybody might feel like going outside.

Paul: Mmm.

Yoko: It's just starting to be great.

Glyn: It's really getting together.

Paul: I think all I want to do is like… having got it together musically, I probably just want to go in and have fun with it, rather than just finish off exactly as we've started. I'd like to sort of do a phwah! for the finish. You know, I'd like to light a rocket and really sort of take off for the end of it. But that's going a bit, like, overboard, I suppose [he shrugs].

John: I think the payoff is us doing great.

What follows shows that the first discussions about the possibility of The Beatles playing on top of the Apple offices are now taking place. Cameras film Paul, Ringo, Mal, Michael, Glyn and Kevin Harrington on the roof, exploring its possibilities: at one point, Paul – assisted by Mal – climbs to its highest part, followed by the others. On the Nagra tapes, an unknown voice asks George Martin, 'Do you know you're up on the roof after lunch?' He replies: 'Yeah, I heard about that.' In the basement, through the afternoon, the group work concertedly on 'For You Blue', before eventually listening to a playback. More work then takes place on 'Let It Be'.

Paul: Can we carry this on tomorrow?
John: Yes, all right.
Paul: I feel sort of a bit tired now, you know… darling [laughs]. You don't mind if we finish now, do you?
John: [comically] I'm just trying to get the group working, you know…
Paul: I know, yes. Office hours. You don't like going home, do you?
John: We don't have to go home.
Paul: No, that's true.
John: We can play… Okay, let's do something else, 'cos we've got an hour, haven't we?
Yoko: Er, we have half an hour.

Led by George, the band fall into Randy Newman's 'Love Story (You And Me)', before playing Duane Eddy's 'Cannonball', and the bluegrass and skiffle standard 'Last Train To San Fernando', before calling it a day.
Paul: Ta-ra, Rich.
Ringo: 'Night, Paul.
John: Have a good weekend.
George: Are we coming tomorrow?
Paul: What?
George: Are we coming in tomorrow?
Paul: Yeah.

SUNDAY
26 JANUARY
1969

Enter Ringo, George and Mal. George plays 'Isn't It A Pity', noticeably faster than the version that will be released on All Things Must Pass.

Mal: You've got some beautiful songs…
George: Morning, Glyn.
Ringo: Morning, Glyn.
George plays 'Window Window'.
Ringo: Did you get to bed last night, Glyn?
Glyn: [laughing] Do I look that bad?
Ringo: [laughing] You look undressed.
George: Just went home, had a wash…
Ringo: All week he's been gradually getting later and later. 'Oh, I went to bed at four, six…' So you just look this morning as if you didn't go at all.
Glyn: Oh, I just had the roof down. That's why I look so shabby. I got to bed about – I think it must have been about two. I was really zonked, though. I know that much.
George: Do you want some toast? Omelette?
Ringo: Yeah, I wouldn't mind.
George: It'd be good if you could come in here and feel how you feel when you're leaving.
Glyn: I'm going through the stage now where I ache all over. [laughs] Have you got there yet?
George: No.
Glyn: Oh, terrible.
George: I keep in trim with…
Ringo: Phyllosan [British chlorophyll

tablets, marketed with the slogan 'Fortifies the over-forties']. By the time we go to do the show, you'll…
Glyn: I'll be on my back, mixing.
George: [to Ringo] Have you written any more words, Ringo, to that one about Picasso?
Ringo: No. Have you heard the Octopus one?
George: No.
Ringo plays piano and sings 'Octopus's Garden'.
George: [plays acoustic guitar] You learnt A minor, then.
Ringo: [plays piano and sings]…
'I'd like to be/ Underneath the sea/ In an octopus's garden in the shade/ It would be nice/ Paradise/ In an octopus's garden in the shade…' That's all I've got.
Ringo and George work on 'Octopus's Garden'. Enter John and Yoko, and George Martin.
John: [to Ringo] What am *I* playing, Richie?
Ringo: Er…
George: [sings and plays]…
'In an octopus's garden by the sea…'
Ringo: [to John] You can be…
John: On bass?
Ringo: [laughs] All right. You will be drums.
John: I'll have to be… Oh, drums, right. I think Paul would want to do drums, wouldn't he, with his strong left arm? I'm not getting on that kit without a ciggie.
Everybody laughs.

Enter Paul, Linda and six-year-old Heather.

John: [to Paul] Hey… did you dream about me last night?

Paul: I don't remember.

John: Very strong dream. We both dreamt about it… Amazing. Different dreams, you know. I thought you must have been there. I mean, I was touching you.

George: Was it sexually oriented?

Paul: Oh, you know, John, don't worry about it.

John: There's nothing to worry about.

George Martin: [to Ringo] Do your song again.

More work on 'Octopus's Garden'.

George: [to Ringo] Was he telling [you] the octopuses got to pick up all the seashells? Do you know about that?

Ringo: Yes. That's why I wrote it, 'cos the gardens… when we were on the

boat in Sardinia, and the octopuses…

George: Do you know about that? They collect all nice-looking things and make a garden around where they are, just with all the groovy things they find. [laughs] It's great.

A few moments later.

Heather: I want to be a doggy.

John: You want to be Dougie?

Heather: Dog.

John: Oh, doggy. Okay.

Heather: We've got some baby kittens. They're only about *that* big.

John: Mmm. Are you going to eat them?

Heather: NO!

John: Lots of people do, you know.

Heather: You can't be eating kittens. They've just been born yesterday…

John: You put pastry round them and you have cat pie.

Heather: A few days they were just

born, weren't they?

John: Oh, well you better wait a week or two before you eat them.

Heather: No. I'm never going to eat them.

John: Aren't you? That's very good.

Heather: I'm going to wait until they've grown up. And one of them's beautiful, like Daddy cat… it's got a big black spot there.

John: Oh, you don't eat them if they have black spots.

Heather: The other one's like a tiger.

John: You don't eat them if they're like tigers either.

Heather: I'm a tame tiger.

Ringo: Are you really? I'm very glad you're a tame tiger.

Heather: 'Cos if I wasn't, then I'd scratch you.

Ringo: You might do that, yes.

Heather: And I might eat *you*.

Ringo: Oooh!

The band listen to a playback of 'For You Blue', before playback and work – accompanied once again by Billy Preston – on 'Let It Be'. Eventually, they fall into a three-chord jam. John and Paul start singing Bob Dylan's 'Like A Rolling Stone', and there is a brief exchange about Aretha Franklin's 'I Say A Little Prayer', before John leads a version of 'Twist And Shout', with Heather contributing to the vocals with long 'aaah' sounds.

John/George: [singing] 'Shake it up baby now/ Twist and shout/ Come on baby now… Come on Heather… Shake it up baby, now (Shake it up, baby, now)/ Twist and shout/ Twist and shout…'
The song starts evolving into something else.

John: [sings] 'Well can you dig it? Yeah?'

Paul: 'Yeah yeah yeah yeah, yeah yeah yeah yeah…'

George: 'Can you dig it, yeah, dig it every evening?'

John: [sings] 'Well you can dig it every time of day or night/ Or afternoon, or evening at teatime, at suppertime, at breakfast time, at dinner time, yeah/ I can dig it even when I'm eating [inaudible]…/ Yes I love it!/ Come on, come and give it…'
Some time later, while Heather is still singing…

John: Come on…

Paul: 'If you've got it, can you dig it, can you dig it, can you dig it up…'

John: 'Like a rollin' stone/ Like a rollin' stone/ Like the FBI/ Like the CIA/ And the BBC/ BB King/ And Doris Day/ Matt Busby/ Dig it, dig it, dig it, dig it/ Dig it…'

The band play spontaneous versions of Little Richard's 'Rip It Up', the rock'n'roll standard 'Shake, Rattle And Roll', Leiber and Stoller's 'Kansas City', Little Richard's 'Miss Ann', Lloyd Price's 'Lawdy Miss Clawdy', 'Blue Suede Shoes', and Smokey Robinson's 'You've Really Got A Hold On Me' and 'The Tracks Of My Tears'. More work follows on 'Let It Be' and then on 'The Long And Winding Road' – which starts to acquire its full-band arrangement, and results in the take used on the final Let It Be *album. The band listen to a playback, after which a discussion about the song ensues, punctuated by Heather and Glyn playing a game of 'Mr and Mrs Sock'.*

Paul: See, the only way I've ever heard it is, like, in my head it's like Ray Charles' band.

George: It would be nice with some brass just to ring the sustaining chord…

Paul: Yeah.

Heather: Mr Sock… Mr Sock? Mr Sock?

Glyn: Er, yes, Mrs Sock.

George Martin: Mmm. It's hardly Beatles mode, really.

Paul: Yeah. We were planning to do it anyway for a couple of numbers just to have a bit of brass and bit of strings.

George Martin: Billy? You know Ray Charles pretty well. If Ray Charles did this, what kind of sound would he have?
No reply is audible on the tape.

Paul: Simple, but full. I don't like it to be bare…

George Martin: No. Right.

Paul: … Just me and the Joanna [rhyming slang for piano].
The day starts to draw to a close…

Paul: Okay. Look, we'll say to everyone, 'Come in at twelve tomorrow,' and so then we'll sort of work till nine-ish.

George Martin: Yeah, but if they come up too early, they'll want to eat about three, or four.

Paul: Yeah.

Heather: Paul, will I be coming tomorrow?

George Martin: It's easier…

Paul: We'll eat about four. But…

we'll get it a bit more together. I'll tell Mal. And we'll get it very together for four o'clock, and we'll have a quick meal for an hour…

Heather: Paul?

Paul: And, right… we'll get Mal to sort of hustle us a bit. [shouts] I said, 'We'll get Mal to hustle us a bit.'

Heather [who is on Paul's shoulders]: Paul?

Paul: Yes?

Heather: Am I going to come with you tomorrow?

Paul: No, you're not coming tomorrow, no. I think you're going to school tomorrow.

Glyn: The point is, when we get in in the morning, everyone sort of breezes in…

Paul: Well, look, we'll say twelve tomorrow and then we'll work later. And we'll start all this week working later.

George Martin: I'm going to have a drink.

Glyn: Hey ho.

Paul: [in background] Say good night.

Heather: I said good night. [shouts] Good night everybody!

Paul: [calls out] See you, Bill. See you tomorrow.

Billy: Okay, mate.

George: See you, Paul.

Heather: See you, George.

George: Bye, Heather.

**MONDAY
27 JANUARY
1969**

Enter Paul, John, Yoko, Billy Preston, Glyn and Neil Aspinall. Paul starts intermittently playing 'Strawberry Fields Forever' at the piano.

Paul: [reading from newspaper in hammy, transatlantic voice] 'Beatle John Lennon hugged Japanese actress Yoko Ono last night and said: "My marriage is over. I am in love with Yoko."'

John: 'Japanese actress' is great.

Paul: '"Of course, my wife and I are not through, legally…" How much does he love Yoko? "Much more than I love the Queen."'

Laughing.

A little later.

John: I have a complaint as a director of Apple.

Paul: Mmm.

John: No bog paper!

Paul: Oh yeah?

John: Terrible disgrace!

Paul: They've got pink upstairs.

John: Have they?

Paul: Yeah.

Glyn: We'll put a stop to that.

Enter George.

Paul: How are you?

John: Two hours' extra sleep, you come clean.

George: Oh, I went to bed very late. I wrote a great song, actually… [enthusiastically] happy and a rocker.

John: It's such a high when you get home… I'm just so high when I get in at night.

George: Yeah, it's great, isn't it?

John: I was just sitting there listening to the last takes: 'What have I had? What have I had today?' You know, I ask her [i.e. Yoko], 'Have we had anything?'

Yoko: You're just high in general.

John: Just want to… wooooaah! I just can't sleep… Have a feel of a little thing here… wooh-de-de-der…

George: I keep thinking, 'Oh I'll just go to bed now,' and then I keep hearing your voice from about ten years ago, saying, 'Finish 'em straight away: as soon as you start 'em, you finish 'em.' You once told me…

John: Oh, the song… But I never do it, though. I can't do it. But I know it's the best.

Paul: [to George] Well, what's it called?

George: I've no title. Maybe you can see a title in it somewhere.

At the piano, George plays 'Old Brown Shoe'.

George: [sings] '… I'm steppin' out this old brown shoe/ And baby I'm in love with you…'

The band listen to playbacks of 'The Long And Winding Road', 'Don't Let Me Down', 'Dig It', and some of the '50s rock'n'roll standards they played the previous day, which are accompanied by enthusiastic clapalongs from George.

George: It was really swinging yesterday!
Glyn: Oh, it's beautiful!

George: It'd be great to hear 'The Beatles' Dance Album'. Just do 'em all start-to-finish… all those…
John: Yeah! 'The Beatles Fab Faves', you know. 'Fab Fave Dance Hits'.

Paul plays 'Oh! Darling'. They then move on to 'The Long And Winding Road'. George then plays 'Old Brown Shoe' ('I like that song – the best out of

all mine that I've done so far') on the piano. Paul joins in on drums with Billy on bass, as he guides them through the song. Paul soon switches to lead guitar, capably playing George's Fender Telecaster upside down. Some time later, Michael starts talking about the prospect of the band playing on the roof, and how he and the crew might film it.

Michael: A helicopter costs between a thousand and twelve hundred pounds.
John: Have it on Paul!
Michael: I think it's great, though…
John: Yes. How much does it cost?
Michael: Between a thousand and twelve hundred.
John: Er, what do you say, lads?
George: Yeah!
Paul: Yes!
John: I mean, it's worth it for [a] last shot coming from like a close-up, and right into the distance.
Paul: [to Michael] Have you checked out if you can do it there?
Michael: Yeah. The problem is, is even if… just listen a minute… The weather forecast is good for Wednesday.
John: Oh!
Laughing.
Michael: Even if… when the show is, we'll do the shot on Wednesday which is up on the roof, and we can get no worse than a 4-shot on the roof out toward London, which I think is worth it.
John: What does the weather do to it?
Michael: If cloud is too low…
Ringo: Or again, what if it rains?
Michael: It's got a big zoom on it, so I'd say it's worth it. Is that a 'yes'? Yes, yes, yes…
All: Yes, yes.
Paul: That's a no-no.
Laughing.

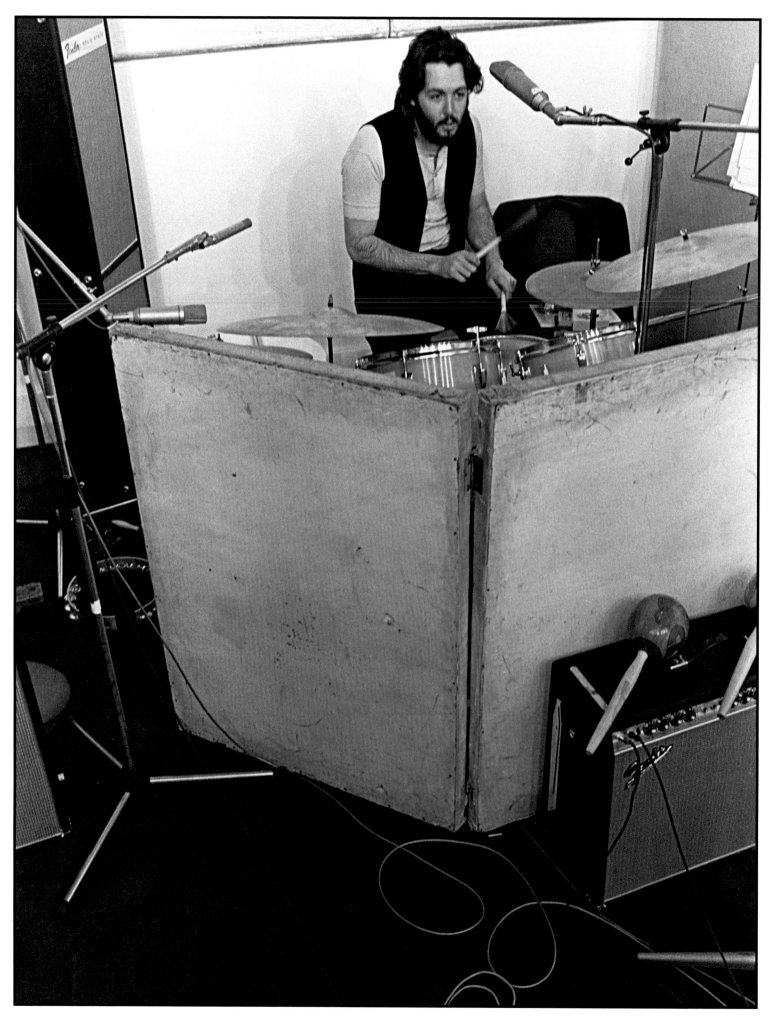

They work on 'Don't Let Me Down' and 'Get Back', and fall into a full-band version of 'Oh! Darling', on which Paul and John harmonise. They then record the take of 'Get Back' that will appear on a single in April and the Let It Be album. Later…

Paul: [sings in broken German] 'Jo Jo war ein Mann das war geschlecht möglich/ Ja das für die ein ganz Kampf/ Aber nach die dags wie da i a mit freundlich/ Ja das für die ungeschaft…

Paul/John: Geh' weg! [giggles] (raus!) Geh' weg! (raus!) Geh' weg! (raus!) nach einer Nacht nach Haus/ Geh' weg! Geh' raus! Geh' raus (raus!) nach irgendeinem Haus/ Geh' raus nach Haus!/ Ja, Jackie…'

Paul: [during solo] 'Ja, Geh' weg, Jackie/ Das war nicht so gut… Geh' weg! Geh' weg! Geht raus nach deinem deinem Haus/ Get back! Geht raus! Geht raus nach neben deinem Haus!/ [speaks] Geh' raus nach deinem Haus! [during solo] Ja, das ist gut, Jackie! Und Zeit mal gut, ja!'

They work on 'I've Got A Feeling', before gathering in the control room.

Paul: We've still got a lot more songs we haven't even rehearsed.

George Martin: Mmm.

Paul: Well, the two slow ones we do, Mother Mary and Brother Jesus…

Laughing.

George: Have we recorded? Have we recorded the Mother Mary one?

Glyn: No.

George: Haven't they?

Paul: Well…

George Martin: The Long, Long Winding one.

Paul: 'The Long And Winding Road'?

Glyn: I think that's very tasty. Très tasty, in fact.

Paul: Oh, the little version we had.

George Martin: He's so good for your morale, this boy. [laughs]

Paul: [laughs] Yeah, yeah.

George: I think one of the best we've done was 'Rip It Up'.

Laughing.

George: It really swung!

They listen to several takes of 'Get Back', culminating in the one that will be included on the Let It Be *album.*

George Martin: We like it. We like that. That had a good ending.

John: Yeah. That wasn't the one where I cocked the solo up.

George Martin: No, that's the next one.

Paul: It's pretty good, that.

George Martin: You were very good, Bill.

Paul: Yeah.

John: What time is it?

George Martin: Just gone half past nine.

A few minutes later.

Ringo: Good night, everybody.

George Martin: Good night, Rich.

John: I think I'm going to go.

Paul: Night, boys.

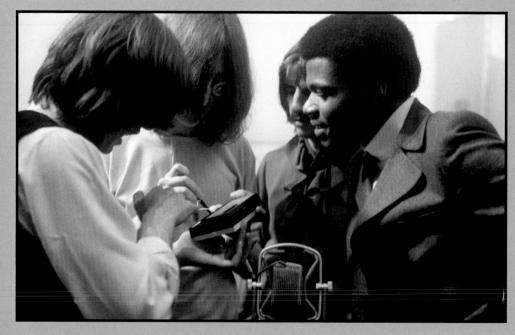

TUESDAY
28 JANUARY
1969

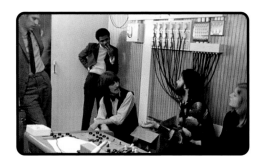

In the control room, Paul, Ringo, John, Yoko, Linda, George Martin, Glyn Johns and Michael Lindsay-Hogg listen to playbacks of some of the songs recorded so far and discuss material recently compiled by Glyn Johns, some of which will eventually go onto his proposed version of an album, entitled Get Back.

Paul: See, listening to the dubs you can really see how incredible they can be, these numbers. But it does tend to need another week of, like, solid rehearsals… Today we should really go through and check whether there's bits we're messing up.
Enter Billy Preston.
Paul: [to Billy] You've got a place. Kings Road. You hear about it?
Billy: No.
Paul: Flat. Kings Road.
Billy: I have?
Paul: Yeah.

Linda: Very trendy.
Paul: [comically] Miniskirts.
Ringo: Service with a smile.
Enter George.
George: Morning, Billy.
Billy: Morning, my man.
Michael: [to George Martin] George, of the ones they've done so far, which do you think we can do on the roof? Anything without the grand piano… Is John going to do 'Can You Dig It'?
George Martin: 'Dig A Pony'?
Michael: Well, he's got another. You know… 'Can you dig it? Can you dig it?'
George Martin: Oh, that one, yeah.
Michael: I would say we could do 'Teddy Boy'…
George Martin: You could do any of those, actually. You could do the ones we've just been listening to.
Michael: 'Get Back'.
George Martin: You see, I think you ought to have the electric piano on the roof.

Michael: Yes, I think so. Well, can we write down what we could do on the roof?
George Martin: [to Alan Parsons, second engineer] Er… you haven't got a concise list of titles – have we, Alan?
Alan: No. I can make one.
Michael: Well, one is 'I Dig A Pony'. We know what we mean by that one, don't we? Do that one on the roof.
Paul: 'Let It Be'.
Michael: 'Let It Be'. Which is 'Let It Be'? Oh no, I think 'Let It Be' needs to be down here.

*The band go on to rehearse
'I've Got A Feeling', at some length.
Paul temporarily leaves. Eventually…*

George: [to Ethan Russell] What's the time? Ethan? What's the time?

Billy: Two-twenty.

George: [to John] I thought you had to go somewhere at one-thirty?

John: No, no. That's Paul [who] had to go somewhere.

George: What did you want to talk about?

John: Well, I'll talk about it when we're doing it. It's just that I saw Klein and that, you know.

George: Who, Klein?

John: Yeah, yeah. Klein. Allen Klein.

George: Oh, I see.

John: Yeah, and it's very interesting.

George: I bet.

John: You know… [quietly] from a lot of angles. But I want to tell you all at once, you know, so as it's not… but I just… I just think he's fantastic.

George: Really?

John: Yeah. But, I mean, I'd just like you to see him, you see, and talk… [There's] a lot of interesting news that we don't know half about, just about…

George: About us?

John: Yeah, you know.

George: Like what?

John: Well, I'll tell… you know, he'll tell you all that, 'cos it's like, you know, [secretively] he knows *everything* about everything.

George: Yeah.

John: On everyone.

George: [laughs] Yeah.

John: You know, he's that big. He's that scale.

George: Yeah.

John: It's like, 'Where's your jet? I'll get it.'… I mean, Alex [Mardas] is always like that too, but you've got to see him, you know.

George: Oh yeah. Okay.

John: Very interesting guy. I was there till two in the morning…

George: Oh, you went last night?

John: I went there thinking, 'Oh fucking hell, well, I've got to see him. I put it off last time.' But I was sort of half-thinking all that time, you know, 'I keep hearing about him all these years, you know. So what? So somebody says he's this or that, you know. What? Said what? About who? What did they say about us? What did they say about Brian?' [strums guitar] But he… fuckin' hell, he knows about Isherwood [Beatles accountant], Bahamas [base of some Beatles finances], Strach [Beatles accountant]…

George: Yeah, well there's…

John: Things that you can't *believe*, you know. The same old news, but right down to *where*: where it's gone, and how to get it. So I didn't really want to say it. I said, 'He's going to look after me whatever,' you know. It's just like that. And he knows, he even knows what we're like, you know, just from the pick-up. I mean, he said he had to see me to know exactly if he was right or not. But the way he described each one of us, you know, and what we'd done and what we're going to do, and that… but just like, you know, I know you, he knows me as much as you do. *Incredible* guy. We [i.e. John and Yoko] were both just stunned. And it was just like, he's one of those guys when he was talking… I mean, so I got the same bit with Ronan [O'Rahilly, founder of Radio Caroline and executive producer of John and Yoko's film *Two Virgins*] and that, but it was never like this.

Yoko: He owns half of MGM.

John: And he's got a great idea for Biafra.

Between July 1967 and January 1970, there was a civil war triggered by the attempted secession from Nigeria of a new state called the Republic of Biafra. The UK government backed Nigeria, whose blockade of the disputed territory led to a huge famine, reckoned to have caused up to two million deaths. Events in Biafra had a major impact all over the world. When John returned his MBE in November 1969, it was partly in protest at the UK's role in this humanitarian disaster.

George: He owns half of MGM?

John: Great idea for Biafra. He's says, 'I'm a practical man…' You know the Stones' *Circus* we did?

George: Mmm.

John: Well, so he arranges those things for them, like…

George: Yeah.

John: All we heard about that, and the royalty from way back…

George: Yeah.

John: They get much more than us. However many we sell, they cop, you know… So, the Stones' show – he's going to make an LP out of it. They're making a book of it, and everything. And he's going to make an LP of it, of everybody that was on, to buy food for Biafra. But not just money, he says. 'Cos you give money to Biafra, or India, [and] he says by the time it's gone through all the…

George: They all take it.

John: Right. So he's going to buy – get this – like the biggest cargo ship in the States. He's got, sort of, chemistry, he owns big chemistry firms, apart from owning MGM…

George: Mmm.

John: … and he's going to sell at cost price all the gear they need, get whoever wants to go, like that… I'd go… from the Stones and the show, and go to Biafra. He says, 'People like you do it, and the whole world, everybody, every kid'll send a halfpenny,' you know. 'Cos he's one of them – like, 'I was an orphan,' you know.

George: [distractedly] Yeah.

Yoko: From an orphanage.

John: When he got on [to talk] about kids, I was like, 'Oh really? You know, you're human. And Biafra…' I said, 'Fuck the rest. Just tell us about the plans for things like that.' You know, so, I mean, that's just great. I was telling him about your idea for that [fundraising] film, and, you know, Presley, he was on…

George: [tuning his guitar] Which one? Oh yeah…

John: … you know, all that, on that scale. He said, 'Presley wouldn't do it.'

George: He would.

John: … 'I don't think Dylan would.' And I said…

George: Dylan will.

John: Dylan will. Okay, okay – this is what he said.

George: Presley will if we will, I know that…

John: I said Dylan wouldn't. But the thing is, I mean, if they can do it on that scale that we did a boat, took the food to that place, with the money we've, that they, those… that they've all earned… Anyway he wants to go, you know. It's not like we get Beatles commission. But if it's that show, every kid in the world would get their parents to send something…

George: You'd have to go there...

John: Make a film of it, of whatever happened, and all that.

George: … in order not to let the politicians take over.

John: Yeah. You know, we'd do it completely – or he'd do it completely himself, arrange it all. All we'd have to do is go there as the people who everybody watches, you know, including the Stones. I didn't mean to get into all this, but he's so fascinating, you know. *Guitars.*

John: Do you want to do this one more time? 'Cos I'd like to learn 'On The Road To Marrakesh' [i.e. 'Child Of Nature'], or something… or '[Mean] Mr Mustard'. Must do another number, I've decided. Shall we do it one more time? Okay.

*The band play 'I've Got A Feeling',
with John on lead vocals. John then
leads them through 'Child Of Nature'.
After Paul returns and Linda begins
taking photographs, they play finished
takes of 'Dig A Pony', 'Get Back',
'Don't Let Me Down' and 'One After
909', as well as a spontaneous version
of 'Love Me Do'. George leads work
on 'Old Brown Shoe'. John then jams
the key verse of 'I Want You (She's
So Heavy)', with Ringo joining in, and
Billy Preston adding a piano part and
vocals. A new tape reel begins with
the band working on 'Something'.*

George: [sings] 'Something in the
way she moves/ Attracts me like a
moth to candlelight… I don't wanna
leave her now/ You know believe and
how/ Du-dern-du-dern-dah… Something
in the way she moves/ Attracts me like
[inaudible]…/ Something in the way
she moves/ I don't wanna leave her
now/ You know I believe and how…'
John: 'Believe in her'?
George: 'I believe and how'.
They stop playing.

George: 'I don't wanna leave her now.
You know I believe, and how…'
John: Oh, I thought it was 'believe
in her'.
Paul: [sings] 'Something in the way
she moves…'
George: What could it be, Paul?…
It's like, I think of what attracted
me at all.
John: Just say whatever comes into
your head each time: 'Attracts me like
a cauliflower' until you get the word,
you know.
George: Yeah, but I've been through
this one, like, for about six months.
John: You haven't had fifteen people
joining in, though.
George: No. I mean just that line.
I couldn't think of anything like a…
John: [sings] 'Something in the way
she moves/ Attracts…' 'Grabs' instead
of 'attracts'.
George: But it's not as easy to say…
John: 'Grabs me like a southern
honky-tonk…'
George/John: [singing] 'Something in
the way she moves/ And like a

la-la-la-la-la…'
John: Grabs me like a monkey
on a tree…
George/John: [singing] 'Something
in the way she moves/ And all I have
to do is think of her/ Something in the
way she shows…'
George: I didn't like moths.
John: Yeah.
Paul: It's a lovely image, a moth.
George: [sings] 'Attracts me like a
pomegranate…' We could have that:
'Attracts me like a pomegranate'.
[laughs]
John/Paul: [singing] 'Something
in the way she moves…'
George: Oh, where's my drink, Mal?
[sings] 'Attracts me like a mo–'
You see, there's the timing on there,
which is quite important.
George/John: [singing] 'Something in
the way she moves/ Attracts me like
a moth to granite…'
George: Pomegranate.
John: Cauliflower.
*George, John and Paul sing the song,
as it stands.*

John: What were the words, the time in that… what are you saying?

George: I was saying: 'Well, did you know who missed the show'… and to a chorus of 'I don't know, I don't know'.

John: [sings] 'What do you know…?' Something like [sings] 'What do you know…'

George: [sings] 'Fancy Joe missed a show…'

The band move on to rehearse 'Get Back', 'Two Of Us' and 'All Things Must Pass'. The day ends with more work on 'I Want You (She's So Heavy)'.

John: Allen Klein's here. Look out!

George: Where's he going to be?

John: Shall we go up to our rooms to talk?

George: Er, Ron's would be nicer, you know.

Ron Kass was head of Apple Records.

John: Okay. It's just there's more stuff in our room. Good night, all. [singing] 'I want you/ I want you so bad…'

WEDNESDAY 29 JANUARY 1969

Enter John and Yoko, Ringo and Glyn.
John: Oh dear. Smashed my knee going out… Didn't half drink a lot yesterday.
Ringo: Mmm.
John: Just woke up this morning with the hangover. Not in my head, just…
Ringo: With my lips, I get it. They dry up and everything.
John: Yeah. And my tongue just like a sort of billiard table. All sort of… alcohol in my blood, tingling. [Strikes a match] I'm hoping to be great tomorrow.
Ringo: We should finish early tonight. Just go through the numbers over and over again, what we're going to do tomorrow [on the roof]. It's only five or six of them.
John: Yeah. And sleep here.
Ringo: And start at twelve… [to John] Did you go on longer with Allen?
John: Yeah. We were talking till about twelve, or half twelve. Went through everything, you know.
Glyn: Have you met Allen before?
John: I met him the other day over here, and I met him at the [*Rock And Roll*] *Circus.*
Glyn: Strange guy, isn't he?
John: I know. He's fantastic, though.
Glyn: He really is very strange. He's very, very clever.
John: Yeah.
A few moments later…
Glyn: He's extraordinary, his capacity… I can't really explain. When you haven't spoken to him for a long time, you'll know exactly what I mean. I don't know if he speaks to you the same way as he does other people – perhaps not, because you're who you are. But he can take anything you say, if he disagrees with it… I don't know… he can convince anybody of anything. I mean, I could say this piano is black, you see, right, and in five minutes…
John: Oh… shit…
Glyn: … he'd have me believing it was green.
Ringo: Mmm.
John: You think it's black!?
Laughing.
Yoko: That's his kick, I suppose, you know, to make this look green, or

something.
Glyn: And he'll ask you a question, and you're halfway through answering it, and if he doesn't like the answer, or if it's not really what he wanted to hear, he'll change the subject right in the middle of a sentence.
Yoko: Oh yeah. I can imagine it, yeah.
Glyn: That bugs me a bit, actually.
Yoko: Mmm.

Enter Michael Lindsay-Hogg.
Michael: Morning, chaps.
Glyn: Hi, Michael.
Michael: Hi, Glyn.
Ringo: Morning, Michael.
Michael: Morning, RS. How many numbers, first, do you think you'll have by tomorrow at one o'clock when we go up on the roof?
Ringo: About six.
Michael: About six. Any sort of routine…?
John: We'll start today.
Ringo: We'll do that today. Get the show ready, I think.
Michael: That's just going to be great. The weather report, we hear, is good. [inaudible] A helicopter from Europe for you tomorrow…
Ringo: Oh.
Michael: Because we could have got a balloon, but that would have cost…
Ringo: What happens if we go on top of the other roof?
Michael: Because it's somebody else's roof? And then we can get had not only for disturbing the peace, and the noise, but also trespassing.
Ringo: Not if we ask them.
Michael: The other thing is that we can… if the police want to come in, which is conceivable, we can stop them for a long time, by either locking the door and making them get a search warrant; and when they get up to the door going onto the roof it'll be locked. And they've got to go down again. And by that time there'll be twelve thousand people in the street…
John: Do you think?
Ringo: Mmm.
John: It'd be a great publicity stunt.

Yoko: Yeah, it's great.
John: And Paul's going off it, you know. Right, so, we'll just do it. And then if we see it, and if it's any good.…
Michael: I mean, you two are still game…
Ringo: Yes, I'm…
John: I'm game for it, yeah, 'cos I mean… let's have a look at it. It won't harm us, you know. It won't harm us to do it. And we can have a look at the rushes and see if…
Michael: And I figure either it'll be good, or it'll be bad…
Laughing.
Ringo: Well, I'd have thought with the helicopter, it could only be good.
Michael: If the wind is blowing the wrong way, how will that affect us? Glyn says…
Ringo: Oh, just cover up…
Michael: Glyn is the one who's going to be fantastic. So on Glyn's head rests about an £8,000 operation. You said it'd be great. But I don't know.
Glyn: Oh God.

John shows Ringo some acoustic guitar techniques by leading him through old Guy Mitchell hit 'Singing The Blues'. The band, Michael, Glyn, George Martin and Tony Richmond soon fall into a long conversation about the prospect of playing on the roof and how the film might end. Paul still seems to favour some kind of performance in the presence of an audience.

Paul: We should sort of just be there and not do it as a show… but invite people to sit in an audience while we do numbers, and we can still do it like this if we want. And it doesn't have to be, 'Pay your two bobs.' [It] could be just, 'Come and see us rehearse.' 'Cos it's the only payoff to this whole thing, you know – I think.

A few moments later…

Tony: Paul, what's the problem? If we've got everything set for tomorrow, we just go ahead and do it, and if you don't like it then we go back and do it the other way.

Paul: Yes, I know… I mean the roof is like too far out… the roof puts us in the open air, not only in the open air, like on a little roof with wind and rain – if it rains.

Ringo: Or sun if it suns.

Paul: Sun if it suns, and gentle if it's gentle.

Michael: If it rains we don't do it at that time.

Ringo: Anyway.

Michael: We've got to have fairly decent weather. Today's a bit cold.

George Martin: What if it's colder than today?

Paul: It's pretty good… If we do an open-air thing, we should learn all the numbers… All the ones that are going to be on the album. It takes a bit more time, you know.

Seated at the centre of a group that also includes Glyn, Michael and George Martin, John and Paul discuss whether traditional albums ought to be The Beatles' sole focus.

Paul: This thing we've entered upon now, we still haven't got any aim for it except an album… again! Our only aim, *ever*, is an album, you know, which is like a very non-visual thing…

John: But albums is what we're doing at the moment, and it is…

Paul: Yeah but I don't know, you know… We're into albums as the four of us but I really think we could be into other things. But every time I talk about it, I really sound like I'm the showbiz correspondent trying to hustle us to do a Judy Garland comeback, you know. But really all I mean is, well, let's change or let's go into, like, a vision studio after we've learnt all of these [songs]. That's just as good as this [i.e. Apple] for sound, that's got the same sort of thing…

John: I think it's daft to move… on this one, you mean?

Paul: It's like we got much better takes after we moved from Twickenham to here.

John: Oh yeah, but I mean here I like, it's like home…

Paul: Yeah, sure, but our takes are getting not as good.

A few moments later…

Paul: There is a show to be had out of what we've got here which is just so incredible – and you don't have to go on the roof. You don't have to go anywhere; you really only have to sing 'em. And combined with the documentary material leading up to it, it's just an unbelievable thing, because you'll have the two elements…

John: No, I think… Tomorrow is meant [to be] the day we do it. Today is, we've got to get the six – or however many numbers – ready so that we can do…

Paul: Yes, but for who is tomorrow the day we've got to do it? Not for me, you know… The easiest way to finish the show is just to sit here for another few days, rehearse all the numbers,

and then, like today, start rehearsing them one after the other and do three numbers at a time. And, like George [Martin] said, get a programme of where we're going to do [it], and what's going to follow what and just start playing them right through… and then just knock it off. And just do it.

George Martin: Like you used to… and have all your titles on your guitar, you know.

John: We're only capable of doing about seven on the rooftop tomorrow… do seven, and then we'll have to do the same again, and do the next seven.

George Martin: So you, you agree in principle. It's just that you say you're not ready.

John: We're not ready, yeah, sure. We're not ready to do fourteen, you know.

Paul: See, originally I would have liked the TV show to have been, say, in here. And the first day we started – see this is where I wanted video, 'cos in my head, all the rest was documentary, and then one day we'd start to say, 'Now we're going do the numbers'… But what I mean is, there'd be a special camera to take that, and the lights would go a bit brighter… and the place would sort of sparkle, you know, whatever.

Michael: Paul, what you're saying…

Paul: The only trouble is, we really have to want to do a show at the end of it; that's the thing; that's the trouble. None of us have an aim… We've got to get that clear, you know: we don't want a payoff show at the end. It's what I was saying to Mal this morning, you know, 'cos he had a dream last night of us doing a show, and he just said it was just incredible. And I said, I would have loved that, you know. I'd love to just play all these numbers at the Saville [Theatre], you know, one afternoon, to some people…

A few moments later…

John: What's your, sort of, practical answer to the problem now regarding tomorrow? I think we'd be daft just to not do it… well, try and do something tomorrow…

Enter George.
George: Sorry I'm late.
John: … even if it's a grand dress rehearsal, and see how it went. Let's look at how we looked, let's look at the rushes. I mean, if it turns out to be half the show, or half the end product, all right. If it doesn't, there's no difference from any other day except for we tried to do them one after the other. And then, you know… I mean, if we had another six weeks…
George: Six weeks?
John: I mean, you know, if we had another month to play with, to really get the fourteen straight off, it'd be nice to still do the seven we've got.
George: I just don't, you know… I think it's going to take months doing it like that. Again, it's just not…
Paul: So how do you think we should do it, then?
George: Record it, you know. And if you can film some while we're recording them at the same time, okay. But just, you know, get it done is the main thing.
Paul: That's how it is. It's like it's a documentary. See, that's what I want to get in my head. Is it a documentary of us doing another album? Which it is. That's what it is, you know.
John: Except, you know…
Paul: That's all right, then… so it isn't a TV show any more, you see. It isn't any of them [i.e. the options previously discussed]. We're not doing a payoff. We're not doing the eleven numbers straight off for an album. We're going have to, sort of, join 'em. We're going to have to do 'em at separate points.
John: Yeah, I agree with that. I think it's disappointing but, all right, we've only got to seven [songs]. Let's do seven.

Paul: Yeah.
John: 'Cos otherwise… we haven't got time to do fourteen, 'cos Ringo's got to go in two weeks, you know. But we might be able to get another seven off by the end of two weeks. I mean, we will, you know. So we'd have to do two sevens.
Paul: I think the only trouble is…
John: Do fourteen.
George: It'd be nice to have a day off…
John: When we've learned the next seven… let's do the whole lot.
Paul: The only trouble is that the only people who need to agree on what it is we're doing is the four of us, and we're the only ones who haven't ever talked about it…
John: Yes.
Paul: … what it is we're doing here. 'Cos we had the meeting before all this, and said, 'TV show'. So until recently, I've thought, 'So it's a TV show, and that's what's going to happen.' So I've been thinking accordingly. And, er, it's an album. That's what I've gotta get in my head. It's an album.
George: It's an album. And all that footage of film [*sic*] which could make about half a dozen films.
Paul: Yeah, but you know what I mean.
George: No, really.
Paul: It's a film of us making an album.
John: Yeah, but that is, that's a visual.
Paul: Yeah. Yeah, no complaints about it. But I've just got to get that in my head…

A few moments later, after Ringo and Yoko have also joined the discussion…
Paul: So what songs have we got? Have we got a sort of list of what we've got, 'cos…

George Martin: A lot of them are… I mean, there's too much of a list there. But there's certainly everything here…
Paul: Okay. [reading] 'I've Got A Feeling', 'Don't Let Me Down', 'Get Back'… 'I'd Like A Love That's Right? ['Old Brown Shoe']'… [continues reading] 'Long And Winding Road', 'Let It Be'… 'For You Blue'… 'Two Of Us', 'All I Want Is You', 'Across The Universe', 'Maxwell's Silver Hammer'…
John: 'One After 909'.
Paul: 'One After 909'.
Paul: [counts] There's thirteen here already that we've run through…
George Martin: There's quite a few that we've taken time and time again.
George: I've got fourteen of my own that we could do in an hour.
Paul: But listen, there's no surprise numbers even in this. I mean, there's nothing that'd throw us to do it straight…
George: What's 'Rocky Road Blues'?
Glyn: There's 'Dig It', as well, which is very long, if you're going to do 'Dig It'.
Paul: Actually, see, that's it! There's thirteen.
Glyn: 'Dig It' would be the first ten minutes, you know.
Paul: We've got 'em all.
Yoko: Great.
George Martin: And I'd like to have a sequence of doing them too, so that you know what you're going to do next, you know.
Paul: Yeah, and then, sort of, do a bit of a sequence, and that.
Michael: But are you ever going to do anything with them all?
Laughing.
Paul: I know.
Michael: I mean… I've got to ask the question, 'cos otherwise should we just

go on filming it until we all leave here?
Ringo: Till we die. [laughs]
Michael: And what are we going to do? I mean, I'm going crazy. I know that's what I'm supposed to do, but I'm really going crazy.
Paul: Yeah.
Michael: Er, I mean I'm happy to go crazy because it runs in the family. *Everybody laughs.*
Michael: But we ought to figure out what we're going to do.
Paul: Well, I'll tell you what, then. Let's… What we are doing, then, is we're still rehearsing, and we'll get it together.
Michael: Right.
Paul: So then… well, we'll collect our thoughts on it; you must collect yours – on what you think you want…
George: You mean, you still are expecting us to be on the chimney with a lot of people, or something like that?
Paul: Yeah… or something.
Michael: Or even on the stage at the Saville, or anything, yeah.
George: Couldn't you just, er…
Paul: Well, anyway, we won't worry about that. Don't give us that one.
Michael: George, George – 'expecting' is not a word we use any more.

'Thinking about'…
Paul: Praying?
Michael: Hoping. Well now, what about the roof tomorrow? Do you want to collectively do that, or not?
Paul: No, well, let's just decide on that, sort of, a bit later. Let's us keep off that.
Michael: Fine. 'Cos we're all set to go for that if you want it or not.
Paul: We'll do the numbers, you know. We're the band.
George: Well, I, you know, whatever. I'll do it if we've got to go on the roof. But, you know, I mean… I don't want to go…
Paul: No, I know…
Michael: You're the band, we're the crew, and never the twain shall meet.
George: 'Course I don't want to go on the roof, you know.
Ringo: I would like to go on the roof.
Paul: You would like to? [laughs]
John: See, I'd like to go on…
Paul: Diverse people. One second.
John: But, I mean, if… see, I don't mind too if anybody doesn't want to go on it, you know.
Paul: That's all right. Anyway, we won't discuss it. That's it. We won't worry about it.
John: And I want to record them as

tracks if you want to record 'em when we're going to, and I want to do it – fourteen numbers, when you want to do it.
Paul: Yeah.
John: 'Cos to me it's all…
Michael: And do it in Africa.
Paul: Any time is paradise when I'm with you. [laughs]
John: Yeah. Any time. Any time at all.
Paul: Yeah. Okay.
Michael: Good. Well, that's settled, then, isn't it?
John: I've said 'yes' to every idea that's come up so far.
Yoko: Right.
John: America, Pakistan, the moon… *Laughing.*
John: You know, I'll still be there singing 'Don't Let Me Down'…
Michael: Me too.
John: You'll be surprised, the stories that come out of this.
George: And it's still that thing of when you go through all [those] hours of footage and start editing it, it'll become whatever it's going to be. It will become it by doing that.
John: I've got great hope, you know.

The band play 'Dig A Pony', 'I've Got A Feeling', 'Don't Let Me Down', 'Get Back', 'One After 909' (which John says he tried to give to The Rolling Stones in 1963 instead of 'I Wanna Be Your Man', 'but they didn't want it'), 'She Came In Through The Bathroom Window', 'Two Of Us', 'Let It Be', 'The Long And Winding Road' and 'For You Blue'.

Paul: [sings] 'Something in the way she moves…' Are we going to do 'Something In The Way She Moves'?

George: I need some words. I mean, if you're going to…

John: Let's do the list [of songs] first.

George: I mean…

John: Let's do this list, and we can do another LP next week, you know.

George: Yeah.

John: I've got a few ready now. Oh, fuck! Let's have another LP. Be about a month, or something. We'll sort the next lot.

Ringo: You can tell us.

Paul: Yeah. You can tell us.

George: I've got sort of a few things.

John: Well, I mean, I've got a few things as well. We can plan it out a bit, you know. But let's say we're going to do one more, we may… And when we've got this album, we'll lay out what the order [is] of things we're going to be doing in the next few months. And then we'll arrange, say, May or June – you know… the next one. As long as we know. If we know that we're going to do the next LP in June, or July, or something, then we can get ready for it, you know.

Paul: [enthusiastically] Yeah.

John: 'Cos this LP is a surprise, really, you know. That's why I'm singing 'One After 909' [laughs], to get on the LP.

Paul: Oh, right.

Another rehearsal of 'All Things Must Pass', followed by tentative work on George's song 'Let It Down'.

George: John… I tell you what I'd like to do after this…

John: Yeah.

George: After this show, you know, I've got so many songs that I've got,

like, my quota of tunes for the next ten years, or albums.

John: Yes.

George: I'd just like to maybe do an album of songs.

John: On your own?

George: Yeah… 'cos it would be nice to get 'em all out the way…

John: Yes. It'd be nice anyway.

George: And secondly just to hear what all mine are like all together.

John: Yeah. You see it's good if we put out an LP and it's all safe that The Beatles are together, but George is doing an album.

George: Oh yeah. But, I mean, it'd be nice too if any of us can…

John: Same as me doing an album…

George: … do separate things, like, as well. That, that way it also preserves this, The Beatle bit of it, more. Because then…

John: You could have an outlet for every little note you want…

George: You know, 'cos all these songs of mine I could give to people who could do 'em good, but I suddenly realised, you know, fuck all that: I'm just going to do me for a bit… you know. [laughs]

Billy: Yes, yes. That's the real thing, man.

Yoko: It's great. That's a good idea.

George: With all these tunes… I could do 'em in a week at the most… 'cos they're all very simple, you know. I mean, I don't think they need much, you know.

Paul's brother Mike arrives. The band fall into a loose jam on 'I Want You (She's So Heavy)', including a spontaneous Billy Preston vocal: 'Oh I had a dream, a very good dream, yes I did/ I had a dream, baby, a very good dream, baby…/ Black or white… I feel alright'. They move on to 'Something' (on which John briefly sings), 'Sexy Sadie', 'Dig It', the version of 'Besame Mucho' seen in the Let It Be *film, 'Three Cool Cats', a slowed-down 'One After 909', Dee Clark's 1959 'Hey Little Girl (In the High School Sweater)', Buddy Holly's 'Maybe Baby' and 'Peggy Sue*

Got Married', a snatch of the early Paul song 'Thinking Of Linking', and Holly's 'Crying, Waiting, Hoping' and 'Mailman, Bring Me No More Blues'. They move on to 'Teddy Boy' and 'Two Of Us', comically sung by John and Paul through clenched teeth.

Paul: [to outro] Goog-gye…

John: Goog-gye… Hello…

Paul: Gottle of geer… [recites alphabet in manner of bad ventriloquist]

John: [without moving his lips] Greta Gargo, Greta Gargo, Greta Gargo, Greta Gargo… Gette Gavis, Gette Gavis.

A few moments later…

John: Shall we all sleep? We're all sleeping at George's tonight to get in the mood.

George: All right.

John: What if we put the ones [i.e. songs] we know in a hat, [and] shuffle them out to see which order we put 'em in?

Paul: I wonder whether Michael will be doing most of them on the roof tomorrow?

Michael: Well, if you can give me the lyrics, I'll study them tonight.

Paul: Yeah, I know. We'll just… we'll back you up.

John: We'll back you up to the hilt.

Paul: Suit tomorrow.

Michael: Thank you.

John: [ventriloquist voice] And you know, Nichael, we're right gehind you.

Michael: [referring to list of songs] Is this the order?

John: No, well that's not, that's the existing, er, cacophony.

Michael: Good, good. What time are we all going to come in, in the morning?

Paul: We'll all be here eleven thirty.

Michael: [expectantly] Eleven thirty.

ACT THREE: THE ROOFTOP

30 JANUARY 1969

JOHN HARRIS

A prescient hint of how the *Let It Be* sessions might conclude was offered by Paul on 7 January, when The Beatles were still at Twickenham. He suggested doing a show 'in a place we're not allowed to do it. You know, like we should trespass, go in, set up and then get moved – and that should be the show… Getting forcibly ejected, still trying to play your numbers, and the police lifting you.' Now, at lunchtime on a dry but cold January day, The Beatles are close to realising that vision, albeit using a location that they own.

The performance on the roof has been timed to coincide with people's lunch hours. By way of preparation, Mal Evans has led the process of building a stage and preparing the group's instruments and amplifiers. Glyn Johns (who will spend the duration of the rooftop performance in the basement, overseeing its recording) and his assistant engineer Alan Parsons have been to a central London Marks and Spencer store to buy women's stockings, so as to wind-proof microphones.

Plans to hire a helicopter to film the show from above have been dropped. The Beatles' performance is to be captured by six cameras – and in the reception area of Apple, there is another camera behind a two-way mirror, put there to document any drama caused by the show. The Beatles and their associates are well aware that the performance might attract the attention of the police, and thereby work as both good PR and a suitable finale to what has so far been filmed. On the surrounding streets, at least two cameras capture passers-by being interviewed about what is unfolding above them.

Right up until the start, there is still uncertainty about whether the performance will actually happen. 'It was moving this way and that way,' Lindsay-Hogg will remember, 'and I wasn't really sure if we were going to go up on the roof or not… and then there's this silence with nothing decided, and then John said in the silence, 'Fuck it – let's go do it.' And that was the vote. And they turned around and walked up that little staircase into history…'

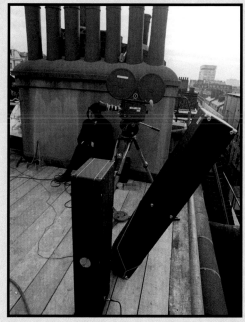

THURSDAY
30 JANUARY
1969

At around 12.30pm, The Beatles and Billy Preston step out onto the roof of 3 Savile Row, accompanied by the crew of people with whom they have been working since early January.

Ringo: Where's the best way, out of the way?
Michael: Over here, I'd think, with Maureen.
Ringo: Sit here. [laughs]
Paul jumps up and down on the newly made stage, to check it's secure.
Michael: [to camera operator] Yeah. Good shot there.
Paul: Where's the instruments?
Ringo: Mal? [laughs] Nailed me [i.e. his drums] down in the wrong place.
Michael: I think, Tony, we'd better cut until the instruments. Cut it!
Ringo: Let's set them up.
Michael: Yeah. Cut it!
Led by John's lead guitar, the band play a snatch of 'Get Back'. Then…

John: Shall we have a go at 'Get Back' then? Shall we try 'Get Back', Paul?
Paul: [sings] 'Jo Jo was a…'
Glyn: Ringo?
John: Whoa… a-hey-hey…
Glyn: [over PA] Ringo? Will you just give us the bass drum? Bass drum, Ringo, when you're ready. Is the mic there?
Ringo: Yeah.
Michael: Glyn. Tell me when you're ready, Glyn.
Glyn: Not yet.
Ringo: [bass drum] How's that?
Glyn: A bit more.
Bass drum.
Glyn: Right. Got it.
John: In the middle we'll do 'Get Back', so take [i.e. record] it.
Glyn: Don't take it.
John: You do. Do take it.
Glyn: Do take it. Right.
John: Come on, youse idiots.
Michael: Get the clapper. Have you got it? Okay.

John: Okay?
George: One, two, three, four…
They play a complete take of 'Get Back', followed by applause.
John: Throwing 'em all…
Paul: Oh thank you very much, you know.
John: Thank you very much.
Paul: It looks like Ted Dexter [English cricketer] has scored another.
John: We've had a request from Martin and Luther…

John plays a snatch of 'I Want You (She's So Heavy)'. Meanwhile, down below…

Man in black raincoat, suit and tie, carrying a parcel: What's happening? What's happening?

Interviewer: The Beatles are doing a free concert on the roof.

Man: Now?

Interviewer: What do you think of it?

Man: I think it's very good. Why aren't they doing it in the street?

Interviewer: They just thought you'd want to hear it.

Man: Yeah, well, we'd also like to see them.

Interviewer: Well, you'd have to pay to go into a hall, so here you don't have to pay anything…

Man: That's true. But why can't they do it on the street?

Interviewer: They'd get pinched.

Man: Well, I think it's a very good thing.

The band play a second take of 'Get Back'.

Interviewer: Excuse me.

Woman, with upper-class accent: Yes?

Interviewer: Do you know what music you're listening to?

Woman: No, I don't.

Interviewer: You don't?

Woman: No.

Interviewer: You don't recognise it at all? Well, that's…

Woman: It's possibly The Beatles.

Interviewer: That's right. It's The Beatles up there.

Woman: Really?

Interviewer: And, er, it's their first public show for some time.

Woman: Oh. You call that public? I can't see them, unfortunately.

Interviewer: You can't see them, no.

Woman: No.

Interviewer: You can't… well…

Woman: So it's not really public viewing, is it?

Interviewer: Er, well…

Woman: It's public *hearing*.

Interviewer: Well, it's public hearing.

Woman: Oh, I see.

Interviewer: And it's the first time that they've played their music openly to the public…

Woman: Yes.

Interviewer: … for quite some time. Are you a Beatle fan?

Woman: Well, you could say so, yes. I think they're great.

Interviewer: You buy their discs, do you?

Woman: No, I don't.

Interviewer: Well, the music that you're now listening to is going to be on their new disc, their new album; it's coming out very shortly.

Woman: Is it? Oh good. Right oh.

A few moments later…

Man with extremely posh accent: Do you know how long this racket is going on?

Interviewer: Er, possibly for about, er, an hour, I think.

Man: You think so?

Interviewer: I would think so.

Up on the roof, they go straight into 'Don't Let Me Down'. On the street, outside the offices of Wain, Shiell & Son, Ltd, a high-end fabrics supplier…

Interviewer: Excuse me. Do you like the music you're hearing at the moment?

Man in light brown overcoat and thick-rimmed glasses, with slicked-back hair: Not particularly.

Interviewer: You don't like it? Why is that?

Man: Well, first of all it's too loud.

Interviewer: It's too loud? Well, the reason for it being loud is to get it across to the public. You see, The Beatles are up there making their first public show for quite some time. And this is to get the music across to, er, all types of people…

Second Man: [shouting] You'll have to speak louder. We can't hear you.

Man: This type of music is all right in its place, so it's quite enjoyable. But I think it's a bit of an imposition to absolutely disrupt all the business in this area.

Interviewer: Do you like normally listening to The Beatles?

Man: In the right surroundings. But definitely not now.

As the band play the versions of 'I've Got A Feeling' and 'One After 909' used on the Let It Be *album, police officers arrive at Apple's front door. The music is very loud, even here.*

Policeman: It's only the police.

Jimmy Clark, Apple doorman: Pardon?

Policeman: Can I have a word with you a minute, please?

A telephone rings.

Policeman: [now inside Apple's reception] Shut the door… We really appreciate this, mate. You know, I don't mind the noise in my [inaudible] personally… but we've had about thirty complaints in the space of half an hour… And what you're doing out there… It's a breach of the peace, all right? You can be taken in for that offence.

Jimmy: Okay. They're just doing, you know, a couple of numbers on the top, that was all. They should be finishing…

Policeman: Okay.

A few moments later…

Policeman: Surely this isn't necessary, is it? I can't really believe that you can't do anything about it.

Debbie Wellum, Apple receptionist: [to policeman] Well, I don't really know. I don't really know what's happening there…

Policeman: I don't, you know, quite honestly… I don't believe that this…

Debbie: But it's some kind of feature that they're doing…

Policeman: Yeah. Well, I don't…

Debbie: … you know, for some film.

Policeman: Yeah. All right. I see that, but you see, I don't really believe this is necessary. Do you?

Debbie: Well, I don't honestly know what they're doing there. I don't know…

Policeman: I think it's ridiculous. You can hear it down by the police station.

Debbie: Really?

Policeman: We've had thirty complaints of noise within minutes, you know.

A door slams twice.

Debbie: Just trying to find Derek [Taylor, Beatles press officer]. Derek?… I can't find him… [coughs]… I didn't know anything was happening on the roof.

'One After 909' ends, and John sings a snatch of the ballad 'Danny Boy'.

Policeman: [into telephone] Can I have CD [Charlie Delta] One Reserve, please? Police?

Mal: Hi. Well, I'm their road manager, The Beatles' road manager.

Policeman: All right, sir, you've got [inaudible]… But this isn't necessary, all right? I mean, we've had thirty complaints at West End Central within minutes.

Mal: Well, really what we're trying to do is [inaudible]…

Policeman: Yeah, I'm afraid... honestly, it doesn't really affect the issue. This has got to go down, otherwise there's going to be some arrests, all right? Now, I'm not threatening you, or anything like that. I'm telling you what's going to happen.

Mal: No. No. I know, I know. We're not trying to antagonise anybody, or…

Policeman: No. Well, can you please…

Mal: Well, you see, we've got a PA speaker up there, you just turn the sound around so they can hear themselves playing, you know.

Policeman: Well, can you turn it off, please?

Mal: Yeah. Okay.

Second Policeman: Turn the PA off. See how it is.

Mal: I think… 'cos I think the instruments themselves won't carry that far.

Second Policeman: Yeah. The thing is, at the moment we can hear it up in [Old] Compton Street.

Policeman: Can you turn the PA off, and we'll see what happens from there.

Mal: Yeah.

Policeman: [exasperatedly] Thank you very much.

Debbie: [to Jimmy Clark] Jimmy?

Jimmy: Hmm?

Debbie: Have a sweet.

Jimmy: Thank you. Don't mind if I do.

Policeman: Aren't these studios soundproofed, or something?

Debbie: It's on the roof!

Policeman: They're on the roof, are they?

Jimmy: Yeah, because they've been recording in the studios, and they've just done this to get some scenery and things, you see.

Debbie: Which is for the big feature I was telling you about.

Jimmy: A big feature film. So…

Policeman: Well, you know, I mean, fair enough…

Second policeman: Well, if you're doing the picture, I'm sure that you can dub the sound onto the film, can't you? The recording?

Debbie: The whole thing is about the live thing, you see. It's got to be live. This is the thing, you see.

The band play 'Dig A Pony', another take that will be selected for the album, as interviews with passers-by continue.

Woman, no older than 25, with chic appearance: Fantastic.

Interviewer: You like it? You really like it, do you?

Woman: Lovely.

Interviewer: You know this is the music to go out on their new album, on their LP?

Woman: When does it come out?

Interviewer: Very shortly. And do you normally buy Beatle music?

Woman: Well, I bought the last LP.

Interviewer: Well, this is the first public show that they've done for quite a while.

Woman: Yeah. So why is it on top of the roof?

Interviewer: Well, it's to do something out of the ordinary. I mean, er…

Woman: [smiling] All that money they've got…

Interviewer: The Beatles have been sort of like space people, you know? So they want to do something extraordinary.

Woman: I see.

Interviewer: That's why the show is done from the roof of the building.

After an improvised version of 'God Save The Queen', the band play further takes of 'I've Got A Feeling', 'Get Back' and 'Don't Let Me Down'. In Apple's reception, the police start asking questions.

Third Policeman: Have you some of our officers in here?

Debbie: Yes, yes.

Third Policeman: Yes?

Debbie: Yes, they're upstairs on the roof.

Third Policeman: Are they really?

Debbie: Yes.

Third Policeman: Much obliged to you. Do you mind if I go in?

Debbie: Erm…

Third Policeman: Would you mind if I go in, madam?

Debbie: Erm, well you can go up, but don't go actually on the roof. It'll probably collapse because it's overweight.

Third Policeman: Thank you.

Debbie: But if you go in the lift to the fourth floor, then that's as far as…

Third Policeman: They've gone up, have they?

Debbie: Yes.

Third Policeman: Thank you very much.

There is a final performance of 'Get Back', just as the police make it onto the roof.

Paul: [singing] 'You been out too long, Loretta!/ You've been playing on the roofs again!/ And that's no good! You know your mommy doesn't like that! She gets angry… She's gonna have you arrested! Get back!'

The song ends, and is followed by applause.

Paul: Thanks, Mo.

John: I'd like to say thank you on behalf of the group and ourselves, and I hope we've passed the audition.

Laughing and more applause.

Later that afternoon The Beatles, Billy, Yoko, Linda, Maureen Starkey, George Martin, Glyn Johns and Michael Lindsay-Hogg are back in the Apple basement, enthusiastically listening to the recording of the rooftop performance.

George: If anybody wanted to play and sing on their roofs, what's the law [to] say why you can't do that?

Michael: I think it…

George Martin: Disturbing the peace.

Michael: Disturbing the peace, because of the PA speakers.

George: Well, how… disturbing the peace? What peace?

Paul: 'Peace' means like noise. You know, they think…

John: Well, they can ban planes, and cars, and…

Michael: Disturbing the peace means traffic jams, people, planes, that sort of thing.

George: We could do it at Hyde Park Corner. That would be allowed.

Playback begins of the rooftop version of 'God Save The Queen', followed by the second take of 'I've Got A Feeling'.

George: I would like what we had yesterday… those big mushrooms. Big fresh, uncut mushrooms.

John: I'll have the same as yesterday: boiled eggs.

George: And cheese. Cheese, boiled eggs…

John: Pancakes and boiled eggs.

George: Can we have hot boiled eggs, Mal? Mushrooms…

They listen to the music.

George: Sounds great.

John: I've been practising on the sly.

The third take of 'Get Back' begins.

George: Oh, that was… this is the one where the police… oh, there was one last time we did 'Get Back' and they were trying to stop us…

John: Yeah.

Playback of the second take of 'Don't Let Me Down'.

George: This is the police now…

Playback of the final 'Get Back'.

George: Are you digging?

John: Yeah. With a bit of doctoring… *Laughing.*

John: … and we'll be goof [*sic*]. I'd say find us a line on 'Don't Let Me Down' [to replace the one he flubbed], use another shot…

Michael: Yeah, quite right.

John: We can trick it up, that.

Paul: Excuse me… called editing, John.

John: We'll edit it, yes.

Paul: [camply] We'll edit it.

George Martin: It's come off actually much better than I thought it would.

Michael: Musically?

Paul: Yeah.

John: [smiling] Just the whole scene is fantastic, you know, just for that scene.

George Martin: But as Michael was saying, you know, this is a very good dry run for something else, too. Apart from the value of this as it stands.

Paul: Yeah.

George: Yeah… for taking over London.

Michael: Yeah.

George: It's a pity it's the wrong time [of year].

Laughing.

George Martin: The idea is you can have a whole squadron of helicopters flying over London, with loudspeakers manned underneath them, you see, *blasting* out the sound when they fly…

John: Fantastic! Yes.

George: And every rock group in the world…

Paul: And us just on the platform just above the speakers…

George: … in London, all over the buildings, playing the same tune.

Paul: Us on a platform of loudspeakers, just sort of strapped into little boxes and just… [sings] 'Weeell, get back', flying over London.

Laughing.

Michael: This will edit fine, 'cos we've got all the cops, which we covered downstairs as well.

John: Great.

Michael: You know, like we got a camera on [them] as they said [things], all that kind of thing. But where we went… the bad things were not enough people in the streets could see us.

George Martin: It'd be marvellous to give a concert filmed from a balloon…

George: Just about twenty bands all in different points over London, it'd have to be closed-circuit TV with each other and… they all start playing at once.

Michael: Seventy-five percent is successful… we can edit it a hundred percent successful… But you're happy now?

Someone makes happy growling noises.

Michael: Is the concert next week? What are you feeling about today? Do you want to work more today, or not?

Paul: [enthusiastically] Yeah. We should record the others now.

Glyn: We've got to get the stuff down first.

Paul: We'll have lunch.

George: We'll have a break for a bit.

Paul: We'll have lunch, and that, and then we record the other stuff that we didn't do up there… acoustic stuff.

Glyn: Up there?

Paul: No. Down here.

George: No, no. There won't be more rooftop singing, 'cos, you know, they really get…

Paul: No, no. No more rooftop. That was the rooftop. That's it.

Glyn: Oh right, yeah.

Paul: But we'll do it down here, only you sort of film it with clappers like the rooftop…

Michael: Yeah.

George: If we got the police, we could pretend in the film that we had to get down because of them, and that here we are in the…

John: [disagreeing] Just the way it happened. It'll just be it, you know.

George: Yeah.

They decide to call it a day, and go home.

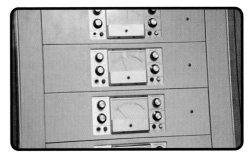 

 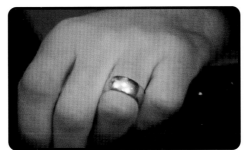

FRIDAY
31 JANUARY
1969

The Beatles and Billy Preston reconvene in the basement of Apple to film and record some of the remaining songs from the last three weeks. After a tongue-in-cheek rehearsal of 'Two Of Us', John leads renditions of Hank Williams's 'Hey Good Lookin'', the American work song 'Take This Hammer', and the US folk standard 'Lost John' (recorded as a single by the skiffle pioneer Lonnie Donegan in 1956). The latter segues into Johnny Cash's 'Five Feet High And Rising', an obscure blues song titled 'Daddy Where You Been So Long?', and 'Right String But The Wrong Yo-Yo', written by the blues musician Piano Red and covered by Carl Perkins. The run of songs ends with The Beatles' own 'Run For Your Life'.

Michael: Do you cats wanna do 'Two Of Us'? Say when, Tony.
John: When, Tony.
Michael: Oh…
John: Good night, Dick.
This was a catchphrase from the US comedy sketch series Rowan and Martin's Laugh-In.
Paul: Good night, Dick… [American accent] Did I ever tell you about when I had [inaudible]…
John: [American accent] I don't think I wanna hear that, Dick.
Paul: Good night, John.
Michael: When the cats are ready.
John: Good night, Paul.
Paul: Say 'Good night', John.
John: Good night, Paul.
Paul: Good night, John.

After a false start, they play 'Two Of Us'.
George: Wasn't it a bit faster?
Paul: Yeah.
George: That was nice faster.
Paul: A bit faster, wasn't it? A bit faster than this?
George: I think so. Just a bit.
Paul: It was.
Paul plays the Italian version of 'Step Inside Love', the song he wrote in 1968 for Cilla Black.
Paul: I'll be all right in a cabaret act when I get older. [sings in French]

'Avec soivez [*sic*]… Avec toi, garçon…' [laughs]
Michael: I mean, are you even…
Paul: His whole life is falling into place, I think you might say.
John: Happiness is a warthog.
Michael: Okay. Get the clapper. Want to do it?
John: Er, poco poco this time, think.
Paul: Poco milliente [*sic*].
John: They're gradually going to freeze us up today, so at the end of the show we're all stiff in ice. It's a sort of finale.
George: It is rather chilly.
John: I think 'rather' is underdoing it.
George: [to bystanders] Do you want to turn the air conditioning off for us?
Michael: Yeah. Jim? Kevin? Can you turn the air conditioning off?

They soon record the take of 'Two Of Us' that will open the Let It Be *album, and move on to 'The Long And Winding Road', interrupted by a spontaneous run-through of 'Lady Madonna', before they return to it, and deliver another complete take.*

John: That was it, wasn't it?

Staring into a camera lens, Paul sharply gasps.

George: Sounded all right.

John: Sounded all right to me.

Ringo: Sounded lovely.

John: Of course, I'm only a commoner.

Paul: What about that last one?

John: Yeah. That was nice, the last one. That was the most…

Paul: [to Glyn] What about it for you? It was the most for us.

Glyn: Yeah.

Paul: It was just the most, man. It sent us.

Glyn: Did it really?

John: We thought, 'Crikey! Burn me!'

Paul: Crikey! Burn me! [laughs] Bun, baby! Bun!

The band play a lengthy jam of 'I Want You (She's So Heavy)', with Paul on vocals. They then move on to several takes of 'Let It Be'.

Glyn: Do you want to do something else?

John: Yeah. Yeah.

Paul: [sings] 'I don't mind.'

Glyn: You could play something else. Would you like to hear something else, whilst you're around?

Derek Taylor: There's one John sang on the roof yesterday which I hadn't heard before…

Michael: 'Route 909'?

Glyn: Oh, it was 'One After 909'.

Michael: Rock'n'roll song.

Glyn: A groover. It's a grooveroony.

Michael: Listen, which ones are we going to do today? I want to know…

Glyn: We're just going to keep going.

Michael: Yeah, but which ones? Hold on.

Paul: Well, let's get 'Let It Be' now.

Glyn: 'Let It Be' is all right.

Paul: The bass. This one.

Glyn: Oh, this is 'Let It Be'. Right.

Michael: Er, so, how close are we to 'Let It Be'?

Glyn: We've got so many takes, there's got to be a good one in there somewhere.

Paul: [clears throat] Okay.

Michael: How close are we to 'Let It Be'?

Glyn: I think about one more take, with John's bass line corrected, and we should be all righty.

Michael: Okay. What would you like to do next, do you think?

Glyn: 'One After 909'.

Paul: We've done that, though, haven't we?

Michael: Yesterday we did 'Don't Let Me Down', 'Get Back', 'I've Got A Feeling', 'One After 909', 'Dig A Pony'. Today we've done 'Two Of Us'. We're about to do one more: 'Teddy Boy', maybe. 'All Things Must Pass' – George's song?

Paul: 'Teddy Boy' is actually, you know… that's as far as it's going to get, unless it really gets written. Isn't it silly?

There's only half a song we've got there.

George: And we haven't got that really to… I haven't learnt that one yet.

Michael: Which one is that?

George: That rocker. You know, that…

Michael: Your song?

George: Yeah.

Michael: Oh, it's great, that. But that's not ready. And 'Teddy Boy' is not ready.

Paul: See, I thought maybe we can come back in, after a week or something.

George: I mean, that last one we've just done, if you just gave us our regular light and took all those things away, we could just do it so much easier. [to Paul] I can just hear in your voice, just not as, you know…

Paul: … relaxed.

George: And it's just not, you know, everybody isn't like *giving*.
A few moments later…
George: Are we going to press on, or are we going to pack up?
Paul: 'Let It Be'. 'Let It Be' again.
Ringo: The Rooftop Beatles rock…
Michael: And, PMcC, after 'Let It Be', do you want to do any more tonight, or not?
Paul: MLH, I don't know yet.
Glyn: 'One After 909'!
Michael: We've done it yesterday, didn't we?
Glyn: Yeah. We'll do it again today for me.
Ringo: [reading from newspaper] 'Paul McCartney shouted, "Don't let me down. I aim to miss the train." [laughs] And The Beatles…'
Unknown voice: That's the same bit as they had in the *Evening Standard*.
Glyn: Well, that's the thing, you see. The *Daily Mail* have got such grotty reporters that they just read the *Evening Standard* the night before and copy whatever they wrote.
Ringo: [reading] 'Mr Davis, 57, director of a clothes wholesaler, said, "All hell was let loose. We are not amused! Work came to a standstill. Our switchboard operators couldn't hear anyone. We said we have had the police in; we have had complaints; but we are not taking any action."' Woah!
Unknown voice: I think they were quite amused…
Ringo: They're young cops, having a bit of a groove.
Glyn: Yeah. They were knocked out…
Ringo: They'd have loved it.
Laughing.

Some time later, after Paul leads a run-through of 'Oh! Darling', they do another take of 'Let It Be'.
Paul: It's the best one.
John: I think that was rather grand. I'd take one home with me.
Glyn: Yeah. That was fine.
John: Don't kid us, Glyn. Give it to us straight… What do you think, Glyn?
Glyn: I think it… Yes!
John: Okay. Let's track it. [gasp of mock-horror] You bounder! You cheat!
Sound of piano and guitar.
John: Get me off this bass! Get me off!

Paul: Was that good enough?
Glyn: Yes.
John: Let's go and hear it, eh, boy?
Paul: Nearly. Well, we'll do one more just to cover ourselves.
George: [We] might play a better one…
John: We've got so many of the bastards to do.
George: One last one, then.
Paul: That's it.
Michael: And include the clapper, please.
John: Oh, clap off!
Sound of guitar.
John: You notice, towards the end of the series, John got a bit strange. [laughs]

Eventually, they deliver the take of 'Let It Be' that will be used – with overdubs – for both the Let It Be *album and the song's release as a single.*
Paul: One more time.
George: Fair. Very fair.
Paul: Very fair. One more…
They play the take of 'Let It Be' that will make it into the film. The tape ends.

AFTERWORD:
WHAT HAPPENED NEXT

JOHN HARRIS

In the wake of The Beatles completing work at Apple Studios on the last day of January 1969, Michael Lindsay-Hogg and his team began editing down around fifty-seven hours of footage, initially with a view to making a film for TV. In early March, Glyn Johns was asked to go through the material recorded at Apple and put together an album provisionally titled *Get Back*. In the meantime, The Beatles had regrouped at Trident Studios in central London, to develop 'I Want You (She's So Heavy)'.

On 11 April, The Beatles released 'Get Back' as a single in the UK, with 'Don't Let Me Down' as the B-side. It spent six weeks at the top of the charts. An accompanying advert in the press said: '"Get Back" is The Beatles' new single. It's the first Beatles record which is as live as can be, in this electronic age. There's no electronic watchamacallit.' In the US, the single was released a month later, and was at the top of the Billboard singles chart for five weeks.

'The Ballad Of John And Yoko' and 'Old Brown Shoe' were recorded in April and released as a single at the end of May, around the same time that Glyn completed work on a finished *Get Back* album. This version included the central spine of the Apple studios material ('Get Back', 'Don't Let Me Down', 'Dig A Pony', 'One After 909', 'I've Got A Feeling', 'For You Blue', 'Let It Be', 'The Long And Winding Road' and 'Two Of Us'), along with a smattering of studio chat. In keeping with its back-to-the-roots spirit, it was decided to turn the artwork into an update of The Beatles' first album, *Please Please Me*. Just as in 1963, the group posed for the cover picture – once again taken by photographer Angus McBean – at the London offices of EMI.

In July, Mal Evans wrote an article for *The Beatles Book* that gave readers a track-by-track account of the album and said it would be released in August. The Beatles, he said, 'would like the film to go on television in August so that everything comes together at the same time.' Michael Lindsay-Hogg finished an initial cut, which was screened in London for The Beatles, their wives, and some of the group's associates on 20 July, the night of the Moon landing. This version was an hour and a half longer than the final cut.

an intimate bioscopic experience with

THE BEATLES

APPLE
An abkco® managed company
presents

"Let it be"

Produced by NEIL ASPINALL   Directed by MICHAEL LINDSAY-HOGG
TECHNICOLOR®

G ALL AGES ADMITTED
General Audiences

United Artists
Entertainment from
Transamerica Corporation

ORIGINAL MOTION PICTURE SCORE
AVAILABLE ON APPLE RECORDS

By this time, The Beatles were immersed in the recording of *Abbey Road*, the release of which – in September – was one of the factors in the *Get Back* film and album being repeatedly pushed back. At around this time, after months of tensions surrounding The Beatles' business dealings and the new involvement in their affairs of Allen Klein, John privately served notice that he was leaving the group, and The Beatles effectively disbanded.

On 3 January 1970, George, Paul and Ringo gathered at Abbey Road Studios to record George's song 'I Me Mine'. Michael's latest cut had included footage of the band working on it, and they wanted to include the full song on the *Get Back* album. Two days later, Glyn finished work on another version of the album, intended to tie in closely with a film that was now being finished for showing in cinemas. The four Beatles could not agree on whether to sign off Glyn's latest work for release – and, in late March, Phil Spector began remixing material from the *Get Back* sessions. He sharply departed from the band's original wish to strip their music back by adding strings, brass and choral voices to 'I Me Mine', the 1968 recording of 'Across The Universe', and – perhaps most egregiously – 'The Long And Winding Road'. *Rolling Stone* magazine called Spector's treatment of this song 'an extravaganza of oppressive mush'.

Paul later said that the first time he heard what Spector had done to the whole album – now retitled *Let It Be*, along with the film – was when it was released.

One month after Paul publicly announced that he had left The Beatles, the album came out on 8 May 1970 in the UK, and ten days later in the USA. The film was premiered in New York City on 13 May, and in London and Liverpool a week later.

In 2003, remixed music from the 1969 sessions was released on the album *Let It Be... Naked*, which was belatedly true to the group's original drive to strip their music down. 'What I like about it is that it's pure,' said Paul. Ringo said this new treatment was 'incredible, really uplifting'. In 2019, it was announced that the film director Peter Jackson was restoring all the unedited footage from January 1969, and working on a new film. He said he was aiming to create an 'experience that Beatles fans have long dreamt about – it's like a time machine transports us back to 1969, and we get to sit in the studio watching these four friends make great music together.'

SONG CREDITS

A Quick One, While He's Away
(Pete Townshend)
TRO – Fabulous Music Ltd

Act Naturally
(Buck Owens)
Sony/ATV Music Publishing LLC

Another Day
(Paul McCartney/Linda McCartney)
MPL Communications, Inc.

Carry That Weight
(Lennon/McCartney)
Sony/ATV Music Publishing LLC

Commonwealth
(Lennon/McCartney)
Sony/ATV Music Publishing LLC

**Da Doo Ron Ron
(When He Walked Me Home)**
(Ellie Greenwich/Jeff Barry/Phil Spector)
© 1963 Universal Songs of PolyGram Int.,
Inc./Trio Music Company/ABKCO Music Inc./
Mother Bertha Music, Inc.

Dig It
(Lennon/McCartney)
Sony/ATV Music Publishing LLC

Don't Bother Me
(George Harrison)
© Universal Songs of PolyGram Int., Inc./Dick
James Music Ltd

Don't Let Me Down
(Lennon/McCartney)
Sony/ATV Music Publishing LLC

**Everybody's Got Something To Hide
Except Me And My Monkey**
(Lennon/McCartney)
Sony/ATV Music Publishing LLC

Get Back
(Lennon/McCartney)
Sony/ATV Music Publishing LLC

Good Rockin' Tonight
(Roy Brown)
Brown Angel Music Publishing (BMI)/Wixen
Music UK Ltd/Wixen Music Publishing, Inc.

I Me Mine
(George Harrison)
Harrisongs Ltd

I've Got A Feeling
(Lennon/McCartney)
Sony/ATV Music Publishing LLC

Just Fun
(Lennon/McCartney)
Lenono Music/MPL Communications, Inc.

Let It Be
(Lennon/McCartney)
Sony/ATV Music Publishing LLC

Madman
(Lennon/McCartney)
Sony/ATV Music Publishing LLC

My Back Pages
(Bob Dylan)
Special Rider Music

No Other Love
(Richard Rodgers/Oscar Hammerstein II)
© 1953 (Renewed) Williamson Music
Company
A Concord Company

Ob-La-Di, Ob-La-Da
(Lennon/McCartney)
Sony/ATV Music Publishing LLC

Octopus's Garden
(Richard Starkey)
Startling Music Ltd
BMG Platinum Songs US/BMG Rights
Management (UK) Ltd

Oh! Darling
(Lennon/McCartney)
Sony/ATV Music Publishing LLC

Old Brown Shoe
(George Harrison)
Harrisongs Ltd

One After 909
(Lennon/McCartney)
Sony/ATV Music Publishing LLC

Picasso
(Richard Starkey)
Startling Music Ltd
BMG Platinum Songs US/BMG Rights
Management (UK) Ltd

Please Mrs Henry
(Bob Dylan)
Dwarf Music

Roll Over Beethoven
(Chuck Berry)
Isalee Music c/o Dualtone Words and Songs
(BMI)/BMG Platinum Songs US (BMI)/
Arc Music Corps

Something
(George Harrison)
Harrisongs Ltd

Taking A Trip To Carolina
(Richard Starkey)
Startling Music Ltd
BMG Platinum Songs US/BMG Rights
Management (UK) Ltd

The Long And Winding Road
(Lennon/McCartney)
Sony/ATV Music Publishing LLC

Twist And Shout
(Bert Russell/Phil Medley)
Sony/ATV Music Publishing LLC/Unichappell
Music/Sloopy II Music/Wren Music Co.,
a Division of MPL Music Publishing, Inc.

Two Of Us
(Lennon/McCartney)
Sony/ATV Music Publishing LLC

3 Savile Row London W.1.

CREDITS

**Photographs by
Ethan A. Russell**
Pages: 3, 4, 6, 10, 15, 19, 21, 26,
28/29, 48, 49, 50/51, 52/53, 54,
55, 56/57, 58, 59, 60, 61, 62, 63,
96, 97, 98/99, 100, 101, 102/103,
104, 105, 106/107, 112, 113, 116,
118/119, 124, 125, 128/129, 130,
131, 132, 133, 138, 139, 140, 141,
142, 143, 144, 145, 146, 147,
148, 149, 150/151, 153, 154/155,
156, 157, 158, 159, 160 (top left),
163 (bottom right), 166, 170, 171,
172, 173, 174, 175, 176, 186, 189,
191, 192, 194, 195, 196/197, 198,
199, 200, 201, 204, 205, 206/207,
208, 209, 210, 211, 214, 215, 218,
219, 220, 221, 222, 223, 224, 225,
226/227, 232/233, 234, 235/236

**Photographs by
Linda McCartney**
Front cover and pages: 22, 23, 74,
75, 76, 77, 78, 79, 80/81, 82, 83,
84, 86/87, 160 (except top left),
162, 163 (except bottom right),
164, 165, 168, 169, 178/179, 180,
182, 183

**Photographs by
Terence Spencer**
Pages: 14, 16, 17

Film Frames
All images with round-cornered
borders are film frames scanned
from the original 16mm footage,
as directed by Michael Lindsay-
Hogg and shot by the 1969
camera crew, including: Anthony
B. Richmond, Les Parrott, Nigel
Cousins, Paul Bond, Mike Fox,
Colin Corby, Mike Malloy, Ronnie
Fox-Rogers, John Holland, Ray
Andrews, Mike Delaney, Terry
Winfield and Roger Boyle

Restoration by WingNut Films and
Park Road Post Production, 2020

Text
Transcribed from the original Nagra
audio tapes as recorded by
the 1969 sound crew including:
Glyn Johns, Peter Sutton, Dave
Harries, Keith Slaughter, Roy
Mingaye and Ken Reynolds

Special Thanks
Paul McCartney
Ringo Starr
Yoko Ono Lennon
Olivia Harrison

Created by Apple Corps
Managing Editor: Jonathan Clyde
Editor: Aaron Bremner
Project Editor: Oliver Craske
Photo Editor: Dorcas Lynn
Art Director: Darren Evans
Audio Tape Transcription:
Emma Montanet and
Olga Sheppard

Callaway Arts & Entertainment
Co-Publisher:
Nicholas Callaway
Managing Editor:
Manuela Roosevelt
Production Director:
True Sims
Production Manager:
Ivan Wong
Production Supervisor:
Toshiya Masuda
Pre-Press Director:
Thomas Palmer
Pre-Press Manager:
Jason Brown

Thanks
Jeff Jones
Garth Tweedale
Neil Mohring
Martin R. Smith
Clare Olssen
Dan Best
Andrew Wylie
James Pullen
Jeremy Neech
Chris Purkiss
Sarah Brown
Steve Ithell
Steve Tribe
All at Apple Corps
All at Callaway Arts & Entertainment

'I'd like to say thank you on behalf of the group
and ourselves, and I hope we've passed the audition.'